LEARN BOSNIAN FOR BEGINNERS

500+ Common Bosnian
Vocabulary and Useful Phrases

SHUK INSTITUTE

TABLE OF CONTENTS

About the Book 1

Target Audience 2

Introduction 4

Chapter One: Letters and Sounds 7

   Alphabets 8

   Vowels 10

   Syllables 10

Chapter Two: Greetings 13

   Introducing Yourself 17

   Vocabulary for Directions 21

Chapter Three: Numbers 24

   Percentages 27

   Fractions 29

   To add 30

To subtract/minus 31

How Much, How Often 33

To Multiply 34

To Divide 35

Chapter Four: Calendar 37

Months Of the Year...38

Days of the week 39

Time...40

Date..45

Chapter Five: Colors 47

Chapter Six: Animals and Insects 49

Chapter Seven: Family and Relations............................55

Chapter Eight: Business 60

Shopping 63

Sentences examples...64

Cost..66

Locations..67

Home..69

Chapter Nine: Technology **72**

    Office 74

    Using a Telephone 76

Chapter Ten: Courtesy and Emergency **79**

Chapter Eleven: What is the Question? **83**

    Asking the Whereabouts of a Person or Thing 85

    Expressing your point of view 87

    Useful Phrases and Structures 88

    Verbs Expressing Your Thoughts 90

    Full Sentence Examples 93

    Well-wishing...94

    Extending Invitations 95

    Example Statements Inviting Someone....................96

    The Hu Tense...97

    Present Tense..100

    Negative Present Tense 101

Chapter Twelve: Action Verbs **103**

    Prefixes - Basics...104

Chapter Thirteen: Other Useful Phrases.......................**109**

Food.. 110

Drinks.. 113

Asking the Time.. 116

Asking the date 117

Asking what somebody is doing 118

Pronouns and copula 119

Saying your nationality.............................. 120

Countries 121

Asking where someone comes from 122

Saying where you are stay / where you reside..... 123

Saying where you live................................ 125

Describing your means of transportation.............. 126

Feeling hungry, thirsty, or satisfied........ 127

Making comparisons................................... 128

Describing an illness................................... 129

Describing how you feel............................. 131

The body.. 132

Chapter Fourteen: Activities 135

Chapter Fifteen: Mini English/Bosnian Travel Dictionary (A-Z) 139

A 140

B...140

C...141

D 142

E...142

F 143

G...143

H 143

I 144

J 144

K...144

L 145

M...145

N 146

O 146

P 147

Q 147

R...147

S 148

T.. 149

U 150

V 150

W 150

X 151

Y 151

Z 151

Conclusion **152**

Review **155**

ABOUT THE BOOK

This book is a quick guide that introduces the reader to the Bosnian language right from its core. It covers a brief history of Bosnian and takes the reader through the language, starting from basic syllables to five hundred essential vocabulary words and phrases. Reading this book will enable English speakers who are beginners to learn and speak Bosnian effectively.

TARGET AUDIENCE

This book is designed for any English speaker interested in learning Bosnian. Students and businesspeople planning to visit Bosnia or any other Bosnian-speaking country for education or business trips will find this book helpful. It caters to a diverse audience, including males, females, children, adults, or any English speaker eager to learn Bosnian.

The book covers basic Bosnian history, fundamental language knowledge, and practical scenarios. Its content helps the reader grasp the language basics and effectively communicate through various phrases in diverse situations.

"To speak a language is to take
on a world, a culture."

– Frantz Fanon

INTRODUCTION

In the heart of Europe, where cultures and civilizations have collided and coalesced over centuries, lies a unique linguistic gem - the Bosnian language. This language, steeped in rich history and cultural nuances, serves as an intriguing subject of study for linguists, historians, and anyone with a passion for understanding the tapestry of human communication.

The Bosnian language, like the country it's named after, is a testament to the profound influence of diverse cultures and historical events. Emerging from the South Slavic family of languages, Bosnian shares its roots with Serbian and Croatian. However, over time, it has carved out its distinct identity. The language's formation process was heavily influenced by the socio-political changes that swept through the Balkans over centuries, from the era of the Roman

Empire to the Ottoman rule and the tumultuous 20th century.

Despite its similarities with Serbian and Croatian, the Bosnian language holds unique features and idiosyncrasies. Its vocabulary is a vibrant mosaic of the different cultures that have touched the land of Bosnia. From Turkish loanwords harkening back to the time of the Ottoman Empire to the influence of Persian and Arabic, the language tells a story of a region that has been a crossroads of civilizations.

Bosnian's official status in the world is an intriguing subject. As one of the three official languages of Bosnia and Herzegovina, it stands alongside Serbian and Croatian. This multilingual characteristic of the country reflects its diverse ethnic makeup and complex history. It's essential to note that while Bosnian is mutually intelligible with Serbian and Croatian, it is recognized as a separate language by several international bodies, including the United Nations. Furthermore, the language is spoken by the Bosniak community in Serbia, Montenegro, and the diaspora around the world.

But what is a language without its cultural signify-cance? The Bosnian language is not merely a medium of communication; it is an embodiment of Bosniak culture and identity. It is a symbol of resilience and survival, a cultural artifact that has withstood the test of time, war, and political upheaval. Its literature, folklore, and poetry are rich tapestries weaving the collective memory and experience of the Bosnian people.

This book aims to delve into the fascinating story of the Bosnian language. As you turn the pages, you will discover the complex process of its formation, its unique characteristics, and its cultural resonance. You will explore the language's historical journey, its official status in the world, and its role in shaping the identity of millions of people.

The Bosnian language, like all languages, is more than a collection of words and grammar rules. It's a living, evolving entity that carries the imprint of its past, shapes the present, and reaches into the future. It's a mirror into the soul of a culture, a nation, and a people. Welcome to this captivating exploration of the Bosnian language, a narrative that promises to be as diverse and multi-layered as the language itself.

CHAPTER ONE:

LETTERS AND SOUNDS

Welcome to a captivating journey through the rhythmic beauty of the Bosnian language! This chapter unravels the tapestry of Bosnian alphabets, vowels, and syllables, each serving as a unique thread in the linguistic fabric of this rich culture. As we delve into the heartbeats of Bosnian - its letters and sounds - we'll discover the magic of a language that echoes centuries of history and tradition. Understanding these foundational elements is like holding a key to a treasure chest, unlocking the intricacies of Bosnian communication. Prepare to be enchanted by the symphony of Bosnian letters and sounds; let's begin!

Alphabets

Immerse yourself in the Bosnian language, a linguistic tapestry rich in history and cultural significance. Its alphabet, a captivating blend of the Latin script, serves as a testament to the country's diverse influences. The Bosnian alphabet consists of 30 mellifluous letters, each carrying its own weight and rhythm. Unlike English, the Bosnian script is phonetic, meaning every letter corresponds to a unique sound, freeing the reader from the complexity of silent letters and unpredictable pronunciations. This enchanting system draws its roots from the Old Church Slavonic language, further shaped by the waves of Ottoman and Austro-Hungarian rule. The Bosnian alphabet is not just a means of communication but also a symbol of resilience and unity in diversity, sparking intrigue with every stroke.

Bosnian Alphabet

A - like "a" in car
B – like "b" in beast
C – like "ts" in cats
Č – like "ch" in chocolate

Ć – like "ch" in church

D – like "d" in down

Dž – like "g" in gin

Đ – like "j" in jack

E – like "e" in let

F – like "f" in fitness

G – like "g" in ground

H – like "h" in heart

I – like "e" in east

J – like "y" in year

K – like "c" in cream

L – like "l" in love

Lj – like "lli" in million

M – like "m" in monarchy

N – like "n" in no

Nj – like "ni" in onion

O – like "o" in old

P – like "p" in pick

R – like "r" in red

S – like "s" in sound

Š – like "sh" in sharp

T – like "t" in time

U – like "oo" in tool

V – like "v" in verb

Z – like "z" in zest

Ž – like "s" in illusion

Vowels

The Bosnian language features five primary vowels: 'a,' 'e,' 'i,' 'o,' and 'u,' each with its unique pronunciation nuances. The 'a' is pronounced like the 'a' in 'father' or 'car' in English. The 'e' is akin to the 'e' in 'pet' or 'red.' Moving on to 'i,' it's comparable to the 'ee' sound in English words like 'see' or 'beet.' The 'o' replicates the 'o' sound in words like 'boat' or 'note.' Lastly, the 'u' mimics the 'oo' in 'boot' or 'moon.' Mastering the pronunciation of these Bosnian vowels can indeed pave the way for a better understanding and command over the language.

Syllables

Syllables in the Bosnian language play a crucial role in shaping its unique pronunciation and rhythm. Unlike English, where syllables are often based on vowel sounds, Bosnian syllables can consist of multiple consonants as well. One fascinating aspect of Bosnian syllables is the potential for intricate consonant clusters that can challenge even the most seasoned linguists.

For example, take the word '**škripa**' (meaning 'squeak' in English). In this word, the syllables are divided as follows: *'š-kri-pa.'* Here, the first syllable contains a single consonant, '**š**,' followed by a consonant cluster '**kri**' in the second syllable, and '**pa**' in the final syllable. This unique combination of consonants creates a distinctive sound that is emblematic of the Bosnian language.

Comparing this to English, we find clear differences in syllable structure. English tends to have simpler syllables, often with just a single consonant or vowel sound. For instance, the English word 'squeak' would be divided into two syllables: 'squeak.' This straightforward division accentuates the distinct vowel sounds in English, whereas Bosnian syllables emphasize the consonant clusters, resulting in a more complex and melodic pattern.

Understanding the intricacies of Bosnian syllables can greatly enhance one's grasp of the language's beauty and rhythm. The fusion of different consonant sounds in a single syllable creates a harmonious flow and adds a certain musicality to spoken Bosnian. It is this unique trait that sets the Bosnian language apart and contributes to its rich cultural heritage.

So, whether you're mastering the intricacies of '**škripa**' or exploring the countless other fascinating syllables in Bosnian, you're embarking on a linguistic journey that intertwines the complexity of consonants with the beauty of its sound. Exploring the world of syllables in the Bosnian language is a true exploration of both linguistic diversity and the human experience.

CHAPTER TWO:

GREETINGS

Your knowledge of a foreign language is essential for interacting with people, especially from a specific origin. This interaction is one of the primary reasons why individuals from different nationalities may want to learn foreign languages, beginning with greetings before delving into other elements such as numbers and additional phrases. Therefore, it's evident that greetings play a critical role in conversations with people from different cultures.

In the previous chapter, you learned about Bosnian letters and sounds, which will aid you in the proper pronunciation of Bosnian words. In this chapter, you will delve into common Bosnian greetings and their translations in English. Recognizing the importance of greetings, which holds true across various cultures, the Bosnian culture being no exception. For instance, greetings set the mood for interpersonal relationships and play a pivotal role in building rapport throughout a conversation.

General greetings to use anytime are:

Greeting: Hello, how are you?
Response: **Dobro, kako ste vi?**
Response: *Doh-broh, kah-koh steh vee?*

Other phrases that you can use as greetings may include:

Welcome to our home / country
Dobrodošli u našu državu
Doh-broh-dosh-lee oo nah-shoo dr-zha-voo

Welcome home (At person's house)
Dobrodošli kući
Doh-broh-dosh-lee koo-chee

Welcome, have a seat!
Dobrodošli, sjednite!
Doh-broh-dosh-lee, syed-nee-teh!

Thank you! / Thank you very much! (Response)
Hvala! / Hvala puno!
Hva -la! / Hva-la poo-no!

Goodbye
Doviđenja
Doh-vee-dyeh-nyah

Goodbye! See you later!
(Response)
**Doviđenja! Vidimo se
kasnije!**
*Doh-vee-dyeh-nyah! Vee-
dee-moh seh kah-snee-yeh!*

Good morning
Dobro jutro
Doh-broh yoo-troh

Good evening
Dobro veče
Doh-br0 vech-e

Good day
Dobar dan
Doh-bar dahn

How are you?
Kako si?
Kah-ko see?

How is everything?
Kako je inače?
Kah-ko yeh ee-nah-che?

What's up?
Šta ima?
Shta ee-ma?

Long time, no see
Nismo se dugo vidjeli
*Nee-smoh seh doo-go vee-
dye-lee*

Excuse me
Izvinite
Eez-vee-nee-teh

Hello, my name is…
Zdravo, moje ime je…
*Zdrah-vo, mo-ye ee-meh
yeh*

See you later
Vidimo se kasnije
*Vee-dee-moh seh kah-snee-
yeh*

See you tomorrow
Vidimo se sutra
Vee-dee-moh seh soo-trah

Let us meet again
Vidimo se opet
Vee-dee-moh seh oh-pet

Have a good day
Ugodan dan
Oo-go-dahn dahn

Have a good night
Laku noć
Lah-koonotch

Sleep well
Lijepo spavaj
Lee-yah-po spah-vay

How is your day?
Kakav je tvoj dan?
Kah-kahv yeh tvoy dahn?

What's new?
Šta ima novo?
Shta ee-ma no-vo?

How is life?
Kako život?
Kah-ko zhee-vot?

Nice to see you
Lijepo te je vidjeti
Lee-yeh-po teh yeh vee-dee-tee

Nice to meet you
Drago mi je da smo se upoznali
Drah-go mee yeh dah smo se oo-poz-na-li

How have you been?
Kako si?
Kah-ko si?

Hello everyone
Zdravo svima
Zdrah-vo svee-ma

How are you feeling?
Kako se osjećaš?
Kah-ko seh os-yeh-chash?

Introducing Yourself

Introducing yourself in the Bosnian language can be an enriching and interesting experience. Bosnian, like any other language, has its unique charm and rhythm. A formal introduction starts with '**Dobar dan**' (Good day), followed by '**Ja sam** [Your Name]' (I am [Your Name]). To express your pleasure in meeting someone, you say '**Drago mi je**' (Nice to meet you). The language is rich in expressions and can be deeply emotive and poetic. Learning Bosnian is more than just acquiring a new language; it's about embracing a vibrant culture.

When meeting someone for the first time, it's best to introduce yourself. Whether in a formal or informal setting, introductions to people who do not know you will most likely start with a greeting. Introductions are some of the scenarios where your knowledge of greetings will be helpful. If you can remember any, for example, '**Zdravo**' meaning 'Hello' would come before your first-time introduction.

My name is…	What is your name?
Zovem se…	**Kako se zoveš?**
Zoh-vem- she	*kah-koh seh zoh-vehsh?*

Pleased to meet you /
Nice to meet you
Drago mi je da smo se upoznali
drah-goh mee yeh dah sahm teh oo-poz-nah-oh

I am from America
Dolazim iz Amerike
doh-lah-zeem eez ah-meh-rih-keh

Where are you from?
Odakle si?
oh-dah-kleh si

Hey, what's up?
Ćao, šta ima?
chow, sh-tah ee-mah?

I am a student
Ja sam student
yah sahm stoo-dehnt

I work for…
Radim za...
rah-deem zah

Nothing special, what about you?
Ništa specijalno, kod tebe?
nee-shtah speh-tsyal-no, kohd teh-beh?

Sometimes, we find ourselves in situations where it's necessary to introduce ourselves. In such cases, here is a list of commonly used sentences for self-introduction.

English	Translation	Pronunciation
Do you speak Bosnian?	**Pričaš li Bosanski?**	*Pree-chash lee boh-sahn-skee?*
Just a little bit!	**Samo pomalo**	*Sah-moh poh-mah-loh.*
No! I don't speak Bosnian. I speak English.	**Ne! Ne pričam Bosanski. Pričam Engleski.**	*Neh! Neh pree-cham boh-sahn-skee. Pree-cham eng-les-kee.*
What is your name?	**Kako se zoveš?**	*Kah-koh seh zoh-vehsh?*
My name is Adam.	**Zovem se Adam**	*Zoh-vehm seh Ah-dahm*
Where are you from?	**Odakle si?**	*Oh-dah-kleh see*
I am from the United States of America.	**Dolazim iz Sjedinjenih Američkih država.**	*Doh-lah-zeem eez s-yeh-dee-nyeh-nih ah-meh-reech-kee dr-zhah-vah.*
When did you arrive here?	**Kada si stigao ovdje?**	*Kah-dah see stee-gah-oh oh-vdyeh?*

I arrived here about two weeks ago.	**Stigao sam prije dvije sedmice.**	*Stee-gah-oh sahm pree-yeh dv-yeh sehdm-eet-seh.*
What do you do for a living?	**Koje je tvoje zanimanje?**	*Koh-yeh yeh tvoh-yeh zah-nee-mahn-yeh?*
I am an accountant.	**Ja sam računovođa.**	*Yah sahm rah-choo-noh-vo-djah.*
Are you here on business or on a visit?	**Jesi li ovdje poslovno ili samo u posjeti?**	*Yeh-see lee oh-vdyeh pohs-lov-noh eel-ee sah-moh u poh-syeh-teh*
I am just visiting.	**Samo u posjeti.**	*Sah-moh u poh-syeh-teh*
I live here.	**Živim ovdje.**	*Zhee-veem oh-vdyeh.*
How many years have you lived here?	**Koliko godina si živio / živjela** (Female) **ovdje?**	*Koh-lee-koh goh-dee-nah see zhee-vee-oh oh-vdyeh?*
I have lived here for six years.	**Živio / živjela** (Female) **sam ovdje šest godina**	*Zhee-vee-oh sahm oh-vdyeh shehst goh-dee-nah.*

How long have you lived here?	**Koliko dugo si živio / živjela** (Female) **ovdje?**	*Koh-lee-koh doo-goh see zhee-vee-oh oh-vdyeh?*
I'm pleased to know you.	**Drago mi je da te poznajem**	*Drah-goh mee yeh dah teh pohz-nah-yem.*
I'm pleased to meet you.	**Drago mi je da sam te upoznao / upoznala** (Female)**.**	*Drah-goh mee yeh dah sahm teh oo-pohz-nah-yoh.*
We will meet later.	**Vidjećemo se kasnije.**	*Veed-yecheh-moh seh kahs-nee-yeh.*

Vocabulary for Directions

Navigating through the charming streets of Bosnia is an exciting adventure, especially when you grasp the basics of the Bosnian language. Understanding directions in Bosnian can be incredibly helpful. Key words such as '**desno**' (right), '**lijevo**' (left), '**ravno**' (straight), '**nazad**' (backwards), and '**okreni se**' (turn around) form the foundation of directional vocabulary. Similarly, phrases like '**gdje je**' (where is), '**kako doći do**' (how to get to), and '**na kojoj strani**' (on which

21

side) can assist in asking for directions. With this vocabulary in your language arsenal, you'll find yourself navigating Bosnia like a local in no time.

Cross the street
Pređi ulicu
preh-jee oolit-soo

Continue down Independence Ave
Nastavi niz Independence Aveniju
nas-ta-vee neez Independence Ave-neh-you

Go straight ahead
Idi samo pravo
ee-dee sah-mo prah-vo

Go down Ghana Avenue
Idi niz Ghana Aveniju
ee-dee neez Ghana Ave-neh-you

Follow this road
Prati ovaj put
pra-tee oh-vai poot

On the first crossroad, turn right
Na prvoj raskrsnici, skreni desno
na prv-oi raskr-sh-nee-tsee, skreh-nee des-no

Other directional terms are:

Crossroad / Junction
Raskrsnica
raskr-sh-nee-tsah

Turn left
Skreni lijevo
Skreh-nee lee-yeh-voh

Turn right
Skreni desno
skreh-nee deh-snoh

Go backwards
Idi nazad
ee-dee nah-zahd

Turn around

Okreni se

oh-kreh-nee she

Go straight

Idi pravo

ee-dee prah-voh

CHAPTER THREE:

NUMBERS

In the previous chapter, you learned about greetings, which will help you kick-start conversations. In this chapter, you will delve into the world of numbers. The Bosnian language boasts a unique number system that is both rich and fascinating. Like English, it uses the decimal system, but the pronunciation and structure of the numbers can be quite distinctive. As you progress, the language continues to be intriguing, with '**jedan**' representing one, '**dva**' for two, and '**tri**' for three. Moving forward, you'll encounter words like '**deset**' for ten, '**dvadeset**' for twenty, and '**trideset**' for thirty. For numbers above this, you simply combine the tens and the units. For example, '**trideset jedan**' is thirty-one. Despite the initial complexity, mastering Bosnian numbers becomes manageable with consistent practice and usage.

0 – Zero	6 – Six
Nula	**Šest**
noo-lah	*shehst*
1 – One	7 – Seven
Jedan	**Sedam**
ye-dahn	*seh-dahm*
2 – Two	8 – Eight
Dva	**Osam**
d-vah	*oh-sahm*
3 – Three	9 – Nine
Tri	**Devet**
tree	*deh-veht*
4 – Four	10 – Ten
Četiri	**Deset**
chay-tee-ree	*deh-set*
5 – Five	11 – Eleven
Pet	**Jedanaest**
peht	*ye-dah-nah-est*

12 –Twelve

Dvanaest

dvah-nah-est

20 – Twenty

Dvadeset

d-vah-deh-set

21 – Twenty-one

Dvadeset jedan

d-vah-deh-set

30 –Thirty

Trideset

tree-deh-set

31 – Thirty-one

Trideset jedan

tree-deh-set ye-dahn

40 – Fourty

Četrdeset

chay-tr-dehst

50 –Fifty

Pedeset

peh-deh-set

60 – Sixty

Šezdeset

sheh-zdeh-set

70 – Seventy

Sedamdeset

seh-dahm-deh-set

80 – Eighty

Osamdeset

oh-sahm-deh-set

90 – Ninety

Devedeset

deh-veh-deh-set

100 – One hundred

Sto

stoh

200 – Two hundred

Dvjesto

d-vyeh-stoh

1,000 – One thousand

Hiljada

heel-yah-dah

100,000 – One hundred thousand
Sto hiljada
stoh heel-yah-dah

100,000,000 – One hundred million
Sto miliona
stoh mee-lee-ohn-ah

1,000,000 – One million
Milion
mee-lee-ohn

10,000,000 – Ten million
Deset miliona
deh-set mee-lee-ohn-ah

1,000,000,000 – One trillion
Milijarda
meel-yee-yar-dah

Percentages

Percentages in the Bosnian language, much like in English, are employed to express a proportion out of a hundred. In Bosnian, the term for percentage is '**postotak**,' pronounced as '*pos-toh-tak*.' When comparing specific percentages between the two languages, you'll notice similarities in their structure. For instance, '25 percent' in English translates to '**25 postotaka**' in Bosnian. The main difference lies in pronunciation and spelling. Additionally, the Bosnian language uses a comma (,) instead of a decimal point (.) to represent fractions in percentages, following a common practice in many European languages. For example, in English, we would write 25.5%, whereas in Bosnian, it would be written as 25,5%.

For example:

1% – One percent
Jedan postotak

2% – Two percent
Dva postotka

3% – Three percent
Tri postottka

4% – Four percent
četiri postotka

5% – Five percent
pet postotaka

6% – Six percent
šest postotaka

23% – Twenty-three percent
dvadeset i tri postotka

7% – Seven percent
sedam postotaka

8% – Eight percent
osam postotaka

9% – Nine percent
devet postotaka

10% – Ten percent
deset postotaka

50% – Fifty percent
pedeset postotaka

100% – One hundred percent
sto postotaka

34.5% – Thirty-four point five
trideset četiri zarez pet postotaka

340% – Three hundred fourty
tristo četrdeset postotaka

Fractions

In the Bosnian language, fractions are expressed in a manner remarkably similar to English, albeit with a distinct Slavic linguistic charm. For instance, the fraction 1/2 is termed '**pola**' (po-lah), akin to the English 'half.' Larger numerals like 3/4 are articulated as '**tri četvrtine**' (*tree chet-vr-tee-neh*), mirroring the English 'three quarters.' The distinctive feature lies in the pronunciation and word order, which differs slightly from English. In Bosnian, the numerator comes first, followed by the denominator, similar to English, but the words for fractions are unique and need to be learned individually. These language intricacies, while distinct, still provide a fascinating link to the universal language of mathematics.

½ – half

Pola

po-lah

⅓ – Third

Trećina

tre-chee-nah

¼ – Quarter

Četvrtina

chet-vr-tee-nah

¾ – Three-quarter

Tri četvrtine

tree chet-vr-tee-neh

To add

Adding, or in Bosnian, '**sabiranje**,' shares similarities with English yet features its own unique characteristics. In both languages, the act of adding involves combining two or more numbers to get a sum. However, the method of expressing this in language differs slightly. In English, the symbol '+' is called 'plus,' and we use the conjunction 'and' to connect the numbers being added. For instance, 'two plus two equals four' translates to '**dva i dva jednako četiri**' in Bosnian. The word 'i' serves as 'and,' while '**jednako**' is the equivalent of 'equals.' Despite these differences in language structure and terminology, the fundamental concept of addition remains universal across all languages, epitomizing the remarkable cross-cultural applicability of mathematical operations.

+ *Plus* (*ploos*)

= *Jednako* (*yed-nah-koh*)

3+2 I **Tri** *plus* **dva** (*tree plus d-vah*)

3+2=5 I **Tri** *plus* **dva** *jednako* **je pet** (*tree plus d-vah yed-nah-koh yeh pet*)

5+3 I **Pet** *plus* **tri** (*pet plus tree*)

5+3=8 I **Pet** *plus* **tri** *jednako* **je osam** (*pet plus tree yed-nah-koh yeh osam*)

To subtract/minus

In the Bosnian language, the term for subtraction is '**oduzimanje**,' pronounced as '*o-du-zi-man-ye*,' which directly translates to 'taking away.' The symbol used is the same as in English, '-'. The term for 'minus' is '**minus**' itself, pronounced as '*mi-nus*.' A sentence such as 'Three minus two equals one' translates to '**Tri minus dva jednako je jedan**' in Bosnian. While both Bosnian and English use the same fundamental concept and symbol for subtraction, the structure of the sentence and the terminology used vary. In English, the operation comes before the numbers ('minus two'), but in Bosnian, it's the opposite ('**dva minus**'). This juxtaposition showcases the beautiful diversity of language while underscoring the universal nature of mathematics.

Examples:

3-2 | **Tri *minus* dva** (*tree minus d-vah*)

5-4 | **Pet *minus* četiri** (*pet minus cheh-tee-ree*)

6-3 = 3 | **šest *minus* tri jednako je tri** (*sh-est minus tree yed-nah-koh yeh tree*)

12-8=4 | **Dvanaest *minus* 8 jednako je četiri** (*Dvah-na-est minus osam yed-nah-koh yeh cheh-tee-ree*)

How Much, How Often

In the Bosnian language, the terms '**koliko**' and '**često**' are used to express 'how much' and 'how often,' respectively. For instance, the phrase '**Koliko jabuka imate?**' translates to 'How many apples do you have?' in English, while '**Idete li često u šetnju?**' means 'How often do you go for a walk?' Interestingly, the structure of these sentences in both languages is quite similar, with the 'how much/many' or 'how often' phrase preceding the verb, just as in English. However, in Bosnian, the verb often comes before the subject, a feature not common in English. For example, '**Koliko knjiga čitate?**' translates to 'How many books do you read?' Here, the verb '**čitate**' (read) comes before the subject '**knjiga**' (books) in the Bosnian sentence. These examples show that while languages may differ in structure and vocabulary, they share the universal ability to ask questions about quantity and frequency, underscoring the wonderful diversity and commonality of human communication.

Once or at once	Twice
Jednom ili odjednom	**Dva puta**
yednom ee-lee od-yed-nom	*dva poo-ta*

Six times	How many books?
šest puta	**Koliko knjiga?**
shest poo-ta	*ko-lee-ko kne-gee-ga*

Seven times	How much?
Sedam puta	**Koliko je?**
se-dam poo-ta	*ko-lee-ko yeh*

How many?	How much sugar?
Koliko?	**Koliko šećera?**
ko-lee-ko?	*ko-lee-ko sheh-cheh-ra?*

How many people?
Koliko ljudi?
ko-lee-ko lyoo-dee

To Multiply

In the Bosnian language, the concept of multiplication is known as '**množenje**' (*mno-zhe-nye*). Just like in English, multiplication is a basic mathematical operation used to increase a number by a certain multiple. The word for 'times'—as in 'two times three'—is '**puta**' (*poo-tah*). So, 'two times three equals six' in Bosnian would be '**dva puta tri je šest**.' The numbers and the structure of the sentence may differ from English, but the fundamental concept remains the same. However, in Bosnian, the structure of the sentence places the numbers before the verb, whereas in English, the verb often comes first in the sentence. Despite the differences in sentence structure and vocabulary, both languages express the idea of multiplication in a way that is simple and easy to understand.

Examples:

2x3 ∣ **Dva** *puta* **tri** (*D-vah poo-tah ter*)

4x4 ∣ **četiri** *puta* **četiri** (*Cheh-tee-ree poo-tah cheh-tee-ree*)

5x6=30 ∣ **Pet** *puta* **šest jednako je trideset** (*Pet puta sh-est yed-nah-koh yeh tree-deh-set*)

3x4=12 ∣ **Tri** *puta* **četiri jednako je dvanaest** (*Tree puta cheh-tee-ree yed-nah-koh yeh dvah-na-est*)

To Divide

In the Bosnian language, the term for 'dividing' is '**dijeljenje**' (*dee-yel-ye-nye*). It's an interesting linguistic comparison when set alongside English. In English, the term 'dividing' is often paired with the word 'by,' as in 'divided by,' which translates to '**podijeljeno sa**' (*po-dee-yel-yeh-no sah*) in Bosnian. However, the Bosnian language often shortens it to '**podijeljeno**' (*po-dee-yel-yeh-no*). The sentence structure differs as well, with the divisor typically following the dividend in English, while in Bosnian, the order generally remains the same. Yet, despite these surface differences, the fundamental mathematical concept of division — breaking down a number into smaller units — is universally consistent.

6÷2=3 ∣ **Šest** *podijeljeno sa* **dva jednako je tri** (*Sh-est poh-dee-yeh-l-yeh-no sa d-vah yed-nah-koh yeh tree*)

30÷3=10 ∣ **Trideset** *podijeljeno sa* **tri jednako je deset** (*Tree-deh-set poh-dee-yeh-l-yeh-no sa tree yed-nah-koh yeh deh-set*)

10÷10 ∣ **Deset** *podijeljeno sa* **deset** (*Deh-set poh-dee-yeh-l-yeh-no sa deh-set*)

50÷21 ∣ **Pedeset** *podijeljeno sa* **dvadeset i jedan** (*Peh-deh-set poh-dee-yeh-l-yeh-no sa dvah-deh-set ee yeh-dahn*)

CHAPTER FOUR:

CALENDAR

The Bosnian language calendar is a fascinating aspect of Bosnian culture, deeply rooted in the country's history and traditions. Unlike the English calendar, which follows the Gregorian system, the Bosnian calendar combines elements of the Gregorian and Islamic lunar calendars. This unique blend reflects the multicultural fabric of Bosnia, where both Christian and Muslim communities coexist harmoniously. The Bosnian calendar features a rich tapestry of religious and cultural festivities, such as Eid, Christmas, and Orthodox Easter, all woven into the fabric of daily life. It is a testament to the diverse heritage of Bosnia, highlighting the country's ability to embrace different beliefs and practices. Understanding the Bosnian calendar is crucial for fully immersing oneself in the vibrant cultural tapestry of this remarkable country. It serves as a guide to the rhythm of life and a window into the soul of Bosnia. In a nutshell, this chapter will help you learn about the months of the year (**mjeseci u godini**), days of the week (**dani u sedmici**), time (**vrijeme**), and date (**datum**).

Months Of the Year

The months in the Bosnian language, like in English, carry a unique significance and rhythm. However, the Bosnian months reflect the country's cultural blend. For instance, January is called '**januar**.' In contrast, February is '**februar**,' symbolizing the harshness of winter. These cultural nuances make the Bosnian language calendar a fascinating exploration of the country's history and traditions. The months are referred to using words that seem borrowed, as follows:

January

Januar

yah-noo-ar

February

Februar

feh-bru-ar

March	August
Mart	**Avgust**
mart	*ov-goost*
April	September
April	**Septembar**
ah-preel	*sep-tem-bar*
May	October
Maj	**Oktobar**
my	*ok-to-bar*
June	November
Juni	**Novembar**
yoo-nee	*no-vem-bar*
July	December
Juli	**Decembar**
yoo-lee	*de-tsemm-bar*

Days of the week

The Bosnian language, like the English language, has seven days of the week. However, the names of the days draw from diverse cultural roots. For instance, Monday in Bosnian is '**Ponedjeljak**,' which means 'the day after Sunday,' compared to English, where it's rooted in Moon's Day. Similarly, Friday is '**Petak**,' meaning 'fifth day,' as opposed to English's 'Friday,' named after the Norse goddess Frigg. These differences in the names of the days between Bosnian and English reflect the unique cultural and historical contexts of the two societies, offering an insightful glimpse into their distinct identities. Here are the days of the week:

English	Translation	Pronunciation
Sunday	**Nedjelja**	*n-ed-yel-yah*
Monday	**Ponedjeljak**	*poh-neh-dyel-yahk*
Tuesday	**Utorak**	*oo-TOH-rak*
Wednesday	**Srijeda**	*SREE-yeh-dah*
Thursday	**Četvrtak**	*CHET-vr-tak*
Friday	**Petak**	*PEH-tak*
Saturday	**Subota**	*SOO-boh-tah*

Time

Time in the Bosnian language has a poetic and symbolic nature that sets it apart from the practical and straightforward English approach. Bosnians refer to time of day with phrases like '**jutro**' for morning, '**podne**' for noon, and '**veče**' for evening, embedding the progression of the day in their language. In contrast, English uses the 12-hour clock system with AM and PM indicators. For example, 7:00 AM is '**sedam ujutro**' in Bosnian, translating directly to 'seven in the morning' rather than just 'seven o'clock.' Similarly, 3:00 PM becomes '**tri popodne**' or 'three in the afternoon.' This difference highlights the cultural nuances between the two languages, with the Bosnian language intertwining the natural rhythm of the day into its timekeeping, and English relying on a more mechanical and universally standardized system. Bosnian time is spoken using words including:

Early morning before dawn
Rano jutro prije svitanja
rah-no yoo-tro pree-ye svee-tah-nyah

From sunrise to a little before noon
Od svitanja do prijepodneva
od svee-tah-nyah do pree-ye-pod-neh-vah

From around noon to around 3PM
Od oko podneva do oko 3 popodne
Od oko pod-neh-vah do oko tree pop-od-neh

From around 3PM to 7PM

Od oko 3 popodne do 7 popodne

od oko tree pop-od-neh do sedam na-ve-chehr

From around 3PM to sunset

Od oko 3 popodne do zalaska sunca

od oko tree pop-od-neh do zalaska soon-tsah

From around 7PM to early morning

Od oko 7 popodne do ranog jutra

od oko sedam pop-od-neh do rah-nog yoo-trah

In the Bosnian language, telling time has its unique charm. For instance, '30 minutes past 3pm' would be expressed as '**pola četiri**,' which directly translates to 'half of the fourth.' This contrasts with English, which uses 'half past three' or 'three-thirty.' For example, 15 minutes past 1pm in Bosnian is said as '**jedan i petnaest**,' meaning 'quarter to two.' In English, it would be 'one-fifteen.' Similarly, 'five minutes to 6pm' in Bosnian is '**pet do šest**,' whereas in English, it's 'five fifty-five.' These examples highlight the unique cultural nuances in how these languages perceive and communicate time.

Here are some of the most important words about 'time' in the Bosnian language:

Century
Vijek
vee-yek

Season
Godišnje doba
go-deesh-nye doh-ba

Clock
Sat
saht

Second
Sekunda
seh-koon-dah

Day / Days
Dan / Dani
dahn / dah-nee

Slow / Slowly
Sporo / Polako
spoh-roh / poh-lah-koh

Day after tomorrow
Prekosutra
preh-koh-soo-trah

Spring
Proljeće
prol-yeh-che

Yesterday
Juče
yoo-che

Sudden
Iznenada
iz-neh-nah-dah

Daytime
Danju
dahn-yoo

Summer
Ljeto
lye-toh

Dusk
Sumrak
soom-rak

Sunrise
Svitanje
svee-tahn-ye

Early
Rano
rah-noh

Sunset
Zalazak sunca
zah-lah-zak soont-sa

Time
Vrijeme
vree-yeh-meh

Hour / Hours
Sat / Sati
saht / saht-ee

Today
Danas
dah-nahs

Late night
Kasna noć
kahs-nah noch

Tomorrow
Sutra
soo-trah

Later
Kasnije
kahs-nee-ye

Watch
Sat
saht

Minute / Minutes
Minuta / Minute
mee-noo-tah / mee-noo-the

Week / Weeks
Sedmica / Sedmice
sed-mee-tsah / sed-mee-tseh

Month / Months
Mjesec / Mjeseci
myeh-sehts / myeh-seh-tsee

What time is it?
Koliko je sati?
koh-lee-koh yeh saht-ee?

Nighttime
Noćno vrijeme
nohch-noh vree-yeh-meh

Winter	Quick / Quickly
Zima	**Brz / brza** (Female)
zee-mah	*brr-zoh / brr-zah*

Now	Yesterday
Sada	**Juče**
sah-dah	*yoo-che*

Year / Years

Godina / Godine

go-dee-nah / go-dee-neh

Date

Speaking dates in Bosnian has a unique charm, as it is rich in cultural context. For instance, '**prvi januar**' means 'first January,' which directly translates to 'January 1st' in English. Furthermore, Bosnians typically say the date first, followed by the month, in contrast to English speakers who typically place the month before the date. To say 'May 31st' in Bosnian, one would say '**trideset prvog maja**.' In contrast, English would simply say 'May thirty-first.' Both languages use cardinal numbers for dates, but Bosnian adds '**og**' or '**i**' to the end, depending on the gender of the noun, signifying the ordinal nature of the date. For example, '11th February 1991' is read as '**jedanaesti februar hiljadu devetsto devedeset prve godine**.'

CHAPTER FIVE:

COLORS

The previous chapter was about the calendar. Congratulations! You are doing well! You are now able to name months of the year, days of the week, and read the date in Bosnian. This chapter will help you learn how to express colors in Bosnian. The table below shows the translation of basic colors. In Bosnian, colors are expressed just as vibrantly as in English, with some slight phonetic differences. For example, 'blue' is '**plavo**,' 'red' is '**crveno**,' and 'yellow' is '**žuto**.' Unlike English, where colors are standalone words, in Bosnian, they often end with 'o' or 'a.' This subtle linguistic variation mirrors the rich and diverse cultural tapestry of the Bosnian language.

English	Translation	Pronunciation
White	**Bijelo**	*bee-yeh-loh*
Gray	**Sivo**	*see-voh*
Black	**Crno**	*tsr-nah*
Brown	**Smeđe**	*s-meh-djeh*
Red	**Crveno**	*tsr-veh-nah*
Orange	**Narandžasto**	*nah-ran-djah-stah*
Yellow	**Žuto**	*zhoo-tah*
Blue	**Plavo**	*plah-vah*
Purple	**Ljubičasto**	*lyoo-bee-chah-stah*
Pink	**Rozo**	*roh-zah*
Gold	**Zlatno**	*zlaht-nah*

CHAPTER SIX:

ANIMALS AND INSECTS

This chapter is one of the most interesting because you will learn animal names in Bosnian. In Bosnian, animals also carry a unique phonetic charm, like colors and dates. For example, a dog is '**pas**,' a cat is '**mačka**,' and a bird is '**ptica**.' These words, while distinct from their English counterparts, still resonate with the same meaning. The most common animals in Bosnia include the brown bear ('**smeđi medvjed**'), wolf ('**vuk**'), and fox ('**lisica**'). These are not only common in the wild, but frequently incorporated into Bosnian folklore and stories, reflecting the bond between Bosnians and their native fauna. Despite the linguistic differences, the appreciation and respect for animals remain universal, whether you're speaking English or Bosnian.

This chapter is one of the most interesting because you will learn animal names in Bosnian. In Bosnian, animal names also carry a unique phonetic charm, similar to colors and dates. For example, a dog is '**pas**,' a cat is '**mačka**,' and a bird is '**ptica**.' These words, while distinct from their English counterparts, still resonate with the same meaning. The most common animals in Bosnia include the brown bear ('**smeđi medvjed**'), wolf ('**vuk**'), and fox ('**lisica**'). These are not only common in the wild but are frequently incorporated into Bosnian folklore and stories, reflecting the bond between Bosnians and their native fauna. Despite the linguistic differences, the appreciation and respect for animals remain universal, whether you're speaking English or Bosnian.

English		Bosnian	
Singular	Plural	Singular	Plural
Animal	Animals	**Životinja /** *zhiv-oh-tee-nyah*	**Životinje /** *zhiv-oh-tee-nyeh*
Ant	Ants	**Mrav /** *mrahv*	**Mravi /** *mrah-vee*
Baboon	Baboons	**Babun /** *bah-boon*	**Babuni /** *bah-boo-nee*
Bear	Bears	**Medvjed /** *med-vyed*	**Medvjedi /** *mehd-vye-dee*
Bird	Birds	**Ptica /** *p-tee-tsah*	**Ptice /** *ptit-seh*
Buffalo	Buffalo	**Bizon /** *bee-zon*	**Bizoni /** *bee-zoh-nee*
Butterfly	Butterflies	**Leptir /** *lehp-teer*	**Leptiri /** *lept-ee-ree*
Cat	Cats	**Mačka /** *ma-chka*	**Mačke /** *mahtch-keh*
Cheetah	Cheetah	**Gepard /** *gehp-ahrd*	**Gepardi /** *geh-par-dee*
Chicken	Chicken	**Kokoš /** *koh-kosh*	**Kokoške /** *koh-koh-sh-keh*
Chimpanzee	Chimpanzees	**Čimpanza /** *chim-pan-za*	**Čimpanze /** *ch-ee-mpan-zeh*
Cockroach	Cockroaches	**Žohar /** *zhoh-har*	**Žohari /** *zhoh-hah-ree*

Cow	Cows	**Krava** / *krah-vah*	**Krave** / *krah-veh*
Crocodile	Crocodiles	**Krokodil** / *kro-ko-deel*	**Krokodili** / *kroh-koh-dee-lee*
Deer	Deers	**Jelen** / *yeh-len*	**Jeleni** / *yeh-leh-nee*
Dog	Dogs	**Pas** / *pahs*	**Psi** / *psee*
Donkey	Donkeys	**Magarac** / *ma-ga-rahts*	**Magarci** / *mah-gahr-tsee*
Duck	Ducks	**Patka** / *paht-kah*	**Patke** / *paht-keh*
Elephant	Elephants	**Slon** / *slohn*	**Slonovi** / *sloh-noh-vee*
Fish	Fish	**Riba** / *ree-bah*	**Ribe** / *ree-beh*
Fly	Flies	**Muha** / *moo-hah*	**Muhe** / *moo-heh*
Giraffe	Giraffes	**Žirafa** / *zhee-rah-fah*	**Žirafe** / *zhee-rah-feh*
Goat	Goats	**Jarac** / *yah-rahts*	**Jarčevi** / *yahr-cheh-vee*
Grasshopper	Grasshoppers	**Skakavac** / *skah-kah-vahts*	**Skakavci** / *skah-kah-vtsee*
Hippopotamus		**Nilski konj** / *nil-skee kony*	**Nilski konji** / *neels-kee koh-nyee*

Horse	Horses	**Konj** / *kony*	**Konji** / *koh-nyee*
Hyena	Hyenas	**Hijena** / *hee-yeh-nah*	**Hijene** / *hee-yeh-neh*
Impala	Impala	**Impala** / *im-pah-lah*	**Impale** / *eem-pah-lah*
Insect	Insects	**Insekt** / *in-sekt*	**Insekti** / *een-sehk-tee*
Leopard	Leopards	**Leopard** / *leh-oh-pahrd*	**Leopardi** / *leh-oh-pahr-dee*
Lion	Lions	**Lav** / *lahv*	**Lavovi** / *lah-vo-vee*
Monkey	Monkeys	**Majmun** / *my-moon*	**Majmuni** / *myah-moo-nee*
Mouse	Mice	**Miš** / *meesh*	**Miševi** / *mee-sheh-vee*
Ostrich	Ostriches	**Noj** / *noy*	**Nojevi** / *noh-yeh-vee*
Parrot	Parrots	**Papagaj** / *pah-pah-guy*	**Papagaji** / *pah-pah-gah-yee*
Peacock	Peacocks	**Paun** / *pow-oon*	**Pauni** / *pah-oo-noh-vee*
Pig	Pigs	**Svinja** / *svee-nya*	**Svinje** / *svee-nyeh*
Python	Pythons	**Piton** / *pee-ton*	**Pitoni** / *pee-toh-nee*

Rabbit	Rabbits	**Zec** / *zets*	**Zečevi** / *zeh-cheh-vee*
Rhinoceros	Rhinoceros	**Nosorog** / *noh-soh-rohg*	**Nosorozi** / *noh-soh-roh-zee*
Shark	Sharks	**Ajkula** / *ay-koo-lah*	**Ajkule** / *ah-koo-leh*
Sheep	Sheep	**Ovca** / *ov-tsah*	**Ovce** / *oh-vtseh*
Snake	Snakes	**Zmija** / *zmee-yah*	**Zmije** / *zmee-yeh*
Tortoise	Tortoise	**Kornjača** / *korn-yah-cha*	**Kornjače** / *korn-yah-cheh*
Turkey	Turkeys	**Ćurka** / *choor-kah*	**Ćurke** / *choor-keh*
Turtle	Turtles	**Kornjača** / *korn-yah-cha*	**Kornjače** / *korn-yah-cheh*
Warthog	Warthogs	**Bradavičasta svinja** / *brah-da-vee-chah-stah svee-nya*	**Bradavičaste svinje** / *brah-da-vee-chah-steh svee-nyeh*
Whale	Whales	**Delfin** / *del-feen*	**Delfini** / *dehl-fee-nee*
Zebra	Zebras	**Zebra** / *zeh-brah*	**Zebre** / *zeh-breh*

CHAPTER SEVEN:

FAMILY AND RELATIONS

Relationships are essential anywhere you go. Bosnian people value relationships with family, friends, and even strangers. In Chapter Two, we learned the importance of greetings in Bosnian culture. Greetings play a crucial role in building relationships among them. In this chapter, you will learn both family and other relationships that exist in Bosnian culture.

Important! The use of terminology varies based on both religious beliefs and personal choices in Bosnian culture and language, owing to the profound influence of Turkish culture. For instance, the term 'Dad' may be referred to as either '**Babo**' or '**Tata**.'

Mother's brother
Dajdža – (Turkism/Muslim)
dy-jah

Ujak – (Others)
oo-yak

Brother / Sister
Brat / Sestra
braht / sehs-trah

Mother
Mama
mah-mah

Brother / Sister-In-Law (Also husband's / Wife's brother)
Zet / Snaha
zet / sna-ha

Mother's elder sister
Starija dajdžinica – (Turkism/Muslim)
stah-ree-yah dy-yee-nee-tsah

Starija tetka – (Others)
stah-ree-yah tet-kah

Child / Children (Plural)
Dijete / Djeca
dee-yeh-the / dyeh-tsah

Mother's younger sister
Mlađa dajdžinica – (Turkism/Muslim)
mlyah-djah dy-yee-nee-tsah

Mlađa tetka – (Others)
mlyah-djah tet-kah

Daughter
Kćerka
kchehr-ka

Nephew / Niece
Nećak / Nećakinja
neh-chahk / neh-chah-kee-nyah

Father
Tata
tah-tah

Paternal Aunt
Tetka
tet-kah

Father-in-law / Mother-in-law
Punac / Punica
poo-nahts / poo-nee-tsah

Paternal uncle
Amidža –
(Turkism/Muslim)
ah-mee-djah

Stric –
(Christians/others)
ah-mee-djah

Female friend / Male friend
Prijateljica / Prijatelj
pree-yah-teh-lee-tsah / pree-yah-teh-ly

Paternal uncle's daughter
Amidžična –
(Muslims/Turkism)
ah-mee-djee-ch-nah

Rodjakinja – (Christians)

Fiancé
Zaručnik – (Male)
zah-roo-ch-neek

Zaručnica – (Female)
zah-roo-ch-neeka

Cousin
Rođak
ro-dyahk

Friend / Friends
Prijatelj / Prijatelji
pree-yah-teh-ly / pree-yah-teh-lyee

Grand-child / Grand
Unuk – (Male)
oo-nook

Unuka – (Female)

oo-nooka

Son

Sin

seen

Grandfather

Dedo –

(Muslims/Turkism)

deh-doh

Djed – (Christians)

deh-doh

Step-father

Očuh

oh-chooh

Grandmother

Nana –

(Muslims/Turkism)

nah-nah

Baka – (Christians)

bah-kah

Step Brother / Sister

Polubrat / Polusestra

poh-loo-braht / poh-loo-sehs-trah

Great grand-child

Praunuk – (Male)

prah-oo-nook

Praunuka – (Female)

prah-oo-nooka

Step-child

Pastorce

pah-stoh-rche

Guardian

Staratelj

stah-raht-ely

Step-mother

Maćeha

maht-cheh-ha

Husband

Muž

moozh

Twins
Blizanci
blee-zahn-tsee

Husband's sister
Prija
pree-yah

Wife
žena
zheh-nah

CHAPTER EIGHT

BUSINESS

Business is part of society. This chapter exposes you to some terms and phrases that might be important in different business settings. Business in the Bosnian language is as diverse and dynamic as in English. In Bosnian, business is referred to as 'posao' (poh-sah-oh). A businessman is '**biznismen**' (*beez-nees-men*), remarkably like English. However, the phrase 'business meeting' translates to '**poslovni sastanak**' (*poh-sloh-vnee sah-stah-nahk*), reflecting the nuances of the language.

In Bosnian, the term 'profit' is '**profit**' (*proh-feet*), and 'loss' is '**gubitak**' (goo-bee-tahk). 'Contract' translates to '**ugovor**' (*oo-goh-vohr*), and 'negotiation' to '**pregovori**' (*preh-goh-voh-ree*). A common phrase in business,

'Return on investment,' is '**povrat na investiciju**' (**poh-vraht nah in-ves-ti-ci-oo**).

Despite phonetic differences, the fundamental aspects of conducting business—negotiations, contracts, profits, and losses—remain universal. Still, the cultural nuances in the Bosnian business landscape add a distinct charm and challenge that may not be present in English-speaking regions.

Business
Posao
poh-sah-oh

Sales
Prodaja
pro-dah-ya

Trade
Trgovina
tr-goh-vee-nah

Price
Cijena
cee-yeh-nah

Profit
Profit
proh-feet

Client
Klijent
klee-yent

Loss
Gubitak
goo-bee-tak

Service
Usluga
oo-sloo-gah

Marketing
Marketing
mar-ket-ing

Competition
Konkurencija
kon-koo-ren-cee-ya

Investment
Investicija
in-vest-ee-see-ya

Gain
Dobit
do-bit

Growth
Rast
ra-st

Advertisements
Oglasi
oh-glah-see

Strategy
Strategija
stra-te-gee-ya

Negotiations
Pregovori
pre-go-voh-ree

Market
Tržište
tr-zhee-shteh

Partnership
Partnerstvo
par-tners-tvo

Tax
Porez
po-rez

Management
Menadžment
men-adzh-ment

Sentences:

My business is in trade
Moj posao je u trgovini
moy poh-sah-oh yeh oo tr-goh-vee-nah

We made a huge profit.
Mi smo ostvarili veliki profit
mee smo ost-var-ili vel-iki proh-feet

We lost due to poor sales

Izgubili smo zbog loše prodaje

iz-goo-bee-lee smo z-bohg lo-she pro-dah-ya

Our price is affordable

Naša cijena je pristupačna

nah-sha cee-yeh-nah yeh pris-too-pah-ch-na

Shopping

Shopping in Bosnian, or '**kupovina**,' is quite like shopping in English. You still have '**prodavnica**' (stores) and '**tržnice**' (markets), just as you have stores and markets in English. However, certain items may be called differently. For example, '**odjeća**' is clothing, '**hrana**' is food, and '**knjige**' are books. While shopping, you might ask '**Koliko košta ovo?**' (pronounced *koh-lee-koh koh-stah oh-voh*), meaning 'How much is this?' It's clear that while the words may sound different, the experience of shopping, the exchange of goods for money, and the interaction with salespeople, is universal, regardless of whether you're in an English-speaking country or Bosnia.

Shopping	To sell
Kupovina	**Prodati**
koo-poh-vee-nah	*pro-dah-tee*
Store	Receipt
Prodavnica	**Račun**
pro-dav-nee-tsah	*rah-choon*
Price	Money
Cijena	**Novac**
tsee-yeh-nah	*no-vats*
Discount	Goods
Popust	**Roba**
poh-poost	*roh-bah*
To buy	Basket
Kupiti	**Korpa**
koo-pee-tee	*kor-pah*

Sentences examples

How much does this cost?
Koliko ovo košta?
ko-lee-ko o-vo kosh-ta?

Where is the nearest store?
Gdje je najbliža prodavnica?
gdye ye nai-bli-za pro-dav-nee-tsah?

Do you have a discount?

Imate li popust?

ee-ma-teh lee poh-poost?

Can I pay with card?

Mogu li platiti karticom?

mo-goo lee pla-tee-tee kar-tee-com?

I want to buy this

Želim kupiti ovo

zhe-leem koo-pee-tee o-vo

This goods is on discount

Ova roba je na popustu

o-va ro-ba ye na po-poost-oo

I can't find what I'm looking for

Ne mogu naći ono što tražim

ne mo-goo nai-chi o-no shto trazh-im

Do you have this in another color?

Imate li ovo u drugoj boji?

ee-ma-teh lee o-vo oo droo-goi bo-yee?

How much money do I have?

Koliko novca imam?

ko-lee-ko no-vats ee-mam?

Please, give me the receipt

Molim Vas, dajte mi račun

mo-leem vas, dai-te mee rah-choon

Cost

In both Bosnian and English, understanding cost is vital when shopping. The Bosnian word for cost is 'cijena.' For example, '**Koliko košta ova haljina?**' (pronounced *koh-lee-koh koh-shta oh-vah hahl-yee-nah*), translates to 'How much does this dress cost?' in English. Similarly, '**Ova knjiga je preskupa**' means 'This book is too expensive.' The concept of cost, whether it's '**cijena**' in Bosnian or 'cost' in English, both terms refer to the universal aspect of trade, crucial for making informed purchasing decisions.

Cost	Cheap
Cijena	**Jeftino**
see-yeh-nah	*yehf-tee-no*
Expensive	Expense
Skupo	**Trošak**
skoo-po	*trow-shak*

Payment	Expenditure
Plaćanje	**Izdatak**
plah-cha-ne	*eez-dat-ak*

Bill	Budget
Račun	**Proračun**
rah-choon	*pro-ra-choon*

Money	Value
Novac	**Vrijednost**
no-vats	*vree-yed-nost*

Discount	Savings
Popust	**Ušteda**
po-poost	*oosh-te-da*

Fee
Naknada
nak-na-da

Locations

In Bosnian, place names or locations are referred to as '**lokacije**.' This is like in English, where we use the term 'locations.' For instance, 'school' in English translates to '**škola**' in Bosnian, while 'home' becomes '**kuća**.' The term 'park' remains the same in both languages. Despite minor differences, the concept of location is universally understood and vital for navigating our surroundings, whether in English or Bosnian.

Market
Prodavnica
pro-dav-nee-tsa

Home
Kuća
koo-cha

Mosque
Džamija
jaa-mee-ya

Bathroom / Toilet
Kupaonica / toalet
koo-pa-oh-nee-tsa / to-a-let

Church
Crkva
tsrk-va

Shower
Tuš
toosh

Shop
Kupovina
koo-po-vee-na

Kitchen
Kuhinja
koo-hee-nya

School
Škola
shko-la

Garden
Dvorište
dvo-ree-shte

Hospital
Bolnica
bol-nee-tsa

Home

In Bosnian, 'home' translates to '**kuća**' or '**dom**.' The concept of home in Bosnian culture is similar to English, where 'house' refers to the physical structure, and 'home' encompasses both the physical and emotional aspects. However, Bosnians often use '**kuća**' to refer to the physical structure and '**dom**' to indicate the emotional connection. For instance, '**Ovo je moja kuća**' translates to 'This is my house,' while '**Ovo je moj dom**' is 'This is my home.' In English, 'house' and 'home' also differentiate the physical and emotional aspects, but the distinction isn't as common in casual conversation. The warmth and security associated with 'home' are universally shared across cultures.

English		Bosnian	
Singular	**Plural**	**Singular**	**Plural**
Bathroom	Bathrooms	**Kupatilo**	*Kupatila*
Glass	Glasses	**Staklo**	*Staklo*
Bed	Beds	**Krevet**	*Kreveti*
Hot		**Vruće**	
Bedroom	Bedrooms	**Spavaća soba**	*Spavaće sobe*

House	Houses	**Kuća**	*Kuće*
Home	Homes	**Dom**	*Domovi*
Bed Sheet	Bedsheets	**Posteljina**	*Posteljine*
Iron Box	Iron Boxes	**Željezna kutija**	*Željezne kutije*
Blanket	Blankets	**Jorgan**	*Jorgani*
Jug	Jugs	**Bokal**	*Bokali*
Bowl	Bowls	**Zdjela**	*Zdjele*
Kettle	Kettle	**Čajnik**	*Čajnici*
Carpet	Carpets	**Tepih**	*Tepisi*
Kitchen	Kitchens	**Kuhinja**	*Kuhinje*
Ceiling		**Plafon**	*Plafoni*
Knife	Knives	**Nož**	*Noževi*
Chair	Chairs	**Stolica**	*Stolice*
Light/ Lamp	Lights/ Lamps	**Svjetlo/Lampa**	*Svjetla/Lampe*
Living Room	Living Rooms	**Dnevni boravak**	*Dnevni boravci*
Cooking Pot	Cooking Pots	**Lonac**	*Lonci*
Mattress	Mattresses	**Madrac**	*Madraci*
Couch	Couches	**Kauč**	*Kauči*
Pan	Pans	**Tava**	*Tave*
Cup	Cups	**Šolja**	*Šolje*
Pillow	Pillows	**Jastuk**	*Jastuci*
Cupboard	Cupboards	**Ormar**	*Ormari*

Plate	Plates	**Tanjir**	*Tanjiri*
Curtain	Curtains	**Zavjesa**	*Zavjese*
Roof	Roofs	**Krov**	*Krovovi*
Dining Room		**Trpezarija**	*Trpezarije*
Saucer	Saucers	**Tanjirić**	*Tanjirići*
Door	Doors	**Vrata**	*Vrata*
Shelf	Shelves	**Polica**	*Police*
Electricity		**Struja**	
Spoon	Spoons	**Kašika**	*Kašike*
Fan	Fans	**Ventilator**	*Ventilatori*
Switch	Switches	**Prekidač**	*Prekidači*

CHAPTER NINE:

TECHNOLOGY

In Bosnian, 'technology' translates to '**tehnologija**.' While the Bosnian language, like English, encompasses a wide range of technological terms, the pronunciation and spelling often differ. For example, 'computer' in Bosnian is '**računar**,' and 'smartphone' becomes '**pametni telefon**.' The word 'internet' remains the same in both languages, testifying to its universal reach. Despite these differences, the concept of technology as a tool for advancement and convenience is identical in both languages. Both Bosnians and English speakers use technology to communicate, learn, and simplify life. It's fascinating to see how universal the concept of '**tehnologija**' is, despite the linguistic differences.

Speaker
Zvučnik
zvooch-neek

Processor (in the computer)
Procesor
proh-ces-or

Screen
Ekran
eh-kran

Monitor
Monitor
mon-ee-tor

Keyboard
Tastatura
tas-ta-too-ra

Mouse
Miš
meesh

Microphone
Mikrofon
mee-kro-fon

Laptop
Laptop
lap-top

Printer
Printer
prin-ter

Mobile Phone
Mobitel
mobee-tel

Internet
Internet
in-ter-net

Email
Email
ee-mayl

Headphones
Slušalice
sloo-sha-lee-tseh

Smartwatch
Pametni sat
pa-met-nee sat

Camera

Kamera

ka-meh-ra

Office

In Bosnian, 'office' is '**ured**' or '**kancelarija**.' Like English, '**ured**' is used to refer to a general workspace, while '**kancelarija**' is often used for more formal, private offices. For instance, '**Moj ured je čist**' translates to 'My office is clean,' and '**Moja kancelarija je velika**' means 'My office is big.' The use and understanding of the term 'office' is quite similar, signifying a space for professional activities. However, the Bosnian language has a bit more specific terms for different kinds of offices, which is not that common in casual English conversation.

English		Bosnian	
Singular	**Plural**	**Singular**	**Plural**
Board (as in 'board of directors')		**Odbor**	
Meeting		**Sastanak**	*Sastanci*
Conference		**Konferencija**	

74

Cabinet	Cabinets	**Ormar**	*Ormari*
Book	Books	**Knjiga**	*Knjige*
Office	Offices	**Ured**	*Uredi*
Messenger		**Vijesnik**	*Vijesnici*
Chair	Chairs	**Stolica**	*Stolice*
Officer	Officers	**Referent**	*Referenti*
Paper		**Papir**	*Papiri*
Clerk	Clerks	**Službenik**	*Službenici*
Pen	Pens	**Olovka**	*Olovke*
Computer	Computers	**Računar**	*Računari*
Pencil	Pencils	**Olovka**	*Olovke*
Computer monitor	Computer monitors	**Računarski monitor**	*Računarski monitori*
Photocopy		**Fotokopija**	*Fotokopije*
Conference room		**Konferencijska sala**	*Konferencijske sale*
Printer	Printers	**Printer**	*Printeri*
Director	Directors	**Direktor**	*Direktori*
Record book	Record books	**Knjiga rekorda**	*Knjige rekorda*
Report	Reports	**Izvještaj**	*Izvještaji*
Fax machine		**Faks uređaj**	*Faks uređaji*
Secretary		**Sekretar**	*Sekretari*

File	Files	**Dokument**	*Dokumenti*
Shelf	Shelves	**Polica**	*Police*
Folder	Folders	**Fascikla**	*Fascikle*
Supervisor		**Supervizor**	*Supervizori*
Janitor		**Domar**	*Domari*
Table/ desk		**Sto**	*Stolovi*
Letter	Letters	**Pismo**	*Pisma*
Manager	Managers	**Menadžer**	*Menadžeri*
Work/job		**Posao**	*Poslovi*
Meeting minutes		**Minute za upoznavanje**	
Worker		**Radnik**	*Radnici*

Using a Telephone

In Bosnian, using a telephone is expressed as '**koristiti telefon**,' which mirrors the English phrase 'using a telephone.' However, the Bosnian language often utilizes the verb '**zvati**' (to call) for most telephone-related activities. For instance, '**Mogu li te zvati?**' translates to 'Can I call you?' in English. Similarly, '**Zovem sa svog telefona**' translates to 'I'm calling from my phone.' It's worth noting that while the English language often differentiates between 'calling' and 'using' a phone, Bosnian tends to use '**zvati**' for both actions, providing a more straightforward approach to telephone-related conversations. However, the nuances of each language's expressions add unique flavors to communication.

Telephone
Telefon
teh-leh-fon

Is there a telephone here?
Ima li ovdje telefon?
ee-mah lee oh-vd-yeh teh-leh-fon

Where is the telephone?
Gdje je telefon?
gd-yeh yeh teh-leh-fon

I want to use a telephone
Želim da koristim telefon
zheh-leem dah koh-ree-steem teh-leh-fon

To call
Zvati
zva-tee

Number
Broj
Broy

Mobile
Mobilni
mo-beel-nee

Call
Poziv
po-zeev

Signal
Signal
see-gnal

Voice
Glas
Glas

Message
Poruka
po-roo-ka

Handset
Slušalica
sloo-sha-lee-tsah

Button
Dugme
doog-meh

Conversation
Razgovor
raz-go-vor

Credit (for prepaid users)
Kredit
kre-deet

Access number
Pristupni broj
pris-too-pee broy

Speaker
Zvučnik
zvooch-neek

Wireless
Bežični
be-zheech-nee

Backlight
Pozadinsko svjetlo
po-za-dins-ko svyet-lo

CHAPTER TEN:

COURTESY AND EMERGENCY

This chapter helps you learn some simple words that you can use during an emergency and shows courtesy. In the Bosnian language, the concept of courtesy and emergency is remarkably similar to what we see in English. For instance, the phrase '**Molim vas**,' meaning 'Please' in English, displays politeness when asking for something. Similarly, in an emergency, '**Hitna pomoć**' translates to 'Ambulance' in English. However, a crucial difference lies in the way these phrases are pronounced, with the Bosnian language relying heavily on diacritical marks. Additionally, Bosnian culture places great emphasis on respect and politeness, so courtesy words are often used even in emergencies. For example, one might say '**Molim vas, trebam hitnu pomoć**,' which means

'Please, I need an ambulance.' This comparison highlights how cultural nuances can influence language use, even in critical situations.

Ambulance	Sorry! (To sympathize)
Hitna pomoć	**Izvinite!**
hit-na po-moch	*eez-vee-nee-the!*
Please	Fire
Molim vas	**Vatra**
mo-leem vas	*va-tra*
Bathroom / Restroom	Get out
Kupatilo / Toalet	**Izaći**
koo-pa-tee-lo / toa-let	*ee-za-chee*
Run away!	Stop
Bježi!	**Stati**
byeh-zhee!	*sta-tee*
Danger	Go away
Opasnost	**Odlaziti**
o-pas-nost	*od-la-zee-tee*
Sorry (To apologize)	Thank you
Izvini	**Hvala**
eez-vee-nee	*hva-la*

Goodbye
Doviđenja
do-vee-jen-ya

Thank you very much
Hvala puno
hva-la poo-no

Help me
Pomozi mi
po-mo-zee mee

Hospital
Bolnica
bol-nee-tsa

Welcome / Come again
Dobrodošli / Dođite opet
do-bro-dosh-lee / do-djee-te o-pet

What?
Šta?
Shta?

How?
Kako?
ka-ko

I'm hurt
Povrijeđen sam
po-vree-yeh-dyen sam

When?
Kada?
ka-da?

I'm sick
Bolestan sam – (Male)
bo-les-tan sam

Bolesna sam – (Female)
bo-les-na sam

Where?
Gdje?
gd-yeh

May I come in?
Mogu li ući?
mo-goo lee oo-chee?

Which?
Koji?
ko-yee

Medicine	No
Lijek	**Ne**
lee-yek	*ne*
Who?	Yes
Ko?	**Da**
ko?	*dah*

CHAPTER ELEVEN:

WHAT IS THE QUESTION?

Questions in the Bosnian language, much like in English, typically begin with interrogative words. For instance, '**Šta**' (What), '**Ko**' (Who), '**Gdje**' (Where), '**Kada**' (When), and '**Zašto**' (Why) are commonly used. While the English language positions the verb before the subject in questions, Bosnian keeps the subject-verb order as in declarative sentences. For example, the English question 'What are you doing?' translates to '**Šta radiš?**' in Bosnian, maintaining the subject-verb order. Though both languages use similar constructs to frame questions, they differ in sentence structure, emphasizing the diversity in language mechanics.

In asking questions about people, things, time, or place, the following words are used:

Who?
Ko?
koh?

What?
Šta?
shta?

Why?
Zašto?
zash-to?

Where?
Gdje?
gd-yeh?

When?
Kada?
kah-dah?

Who are you?
Ko si ti?
koh see tee?

Whose?
Čiji – (male) / **Čija?** –
(Female)
chee-yee? / chee-yah?

Whose child?
Čije dijete?
chee-yeh dee-yeh-teh?

Whose children?
Čija djeca?
chee-yah djet-sah?

Whose book?
Čija knjiga?
chee-yah knjee-gah?

Whose books?
Čije knjige?
chee-yeh knjee-geh?

What did he say?
Šta je rekao?
shta yeh reh-kao?

Where are you going?
Gdje ideš?
gd-yeh ee-desh?

Here
Ovdje
ov-dye

Who is here?

Ko je ovdje?

koh yeh ov-dye?

Come here

Dođi ovdje

dod-jee ov-dye

When did he come here?

Kada je došao ovdje?

kah-dah yeh doh-shao ov-dye?

Why are you laughing?

Zašto se smiješ

zash-to se smee-esh?

Why are you going?

Zašto ideš?

zash-to ee-desh?

Because

Zato

zah-to

I am laughing because I am happy

Smijem se, jer sam sretan – (Male)

smee-yem seh yehr sahm sreht-an

Smijem se, jer sam sretna – (Female)

smee-yem seh yehr sahm sret-nah

Asking the Whereabouts of a Person or Thing

In the Bosnian language, inquiries about the location of a person or object often involve the word 'gdje,' which is equivalent to 'where' in English. For instance, '**Gdje je moj telefon?**' translates to 'Where is my phone?' In English, the structure is Subject-Verb-Object, while in Bosnian, it is often Verb-Subject-Object. However, both languages share a common need for context. For example, '**Gdje je Ana?**' and 'Where is Ana?' both require knowledge of who Ana is. Despite the difference in structure, the intent remains the same, emphasizing the universal human desire for information.

Where is the railway station?
Gdje je željeznička stanica?
gd-yeh yeh zhel-yez-nich-ka stah-nee-tsa?

Where is the teacher?
Gdje je učitelj?
gd-yeh yeh oo-chee-te-lyeh?

Where are the students?
Gdje su učenici?
gd-yeh soo stoo-den-tee?

It is in front
Ispred je
is-pred yeh

He / She's at school
On – (Male) / **Ona** – (Female) **je u školi**
on yeh oo shkoh-lee / ona yeh oo shkoh-lee

They're at home
Oni su u kući

oni soo oo koo-chee

Expressing your point of view

Expressing your point of view in Bosnian, like in English, requires clarity and directness. In Bosnian, you might say, '**Po mom mišljenju, ovo je najbolji način,**' translated to 'In my opinion, this is the best way.' In English, this sentiment is expressed with a similar phrase, 'In my opinion, this is the best way.' Both languages value the speaker's perspective but may differ in tonal nuances. For instance, Bosnian might sound more formal due to its rich morphological structure, while English could appear more casual due to its simpler syntax. Regardless, both languages effectively convey personal viewpoints.

Some useful verbs:

Agree
Složiti se
sloh-zhee-tee she

Disagree or oppose
Ne složiti se
neh sloh-zhee-tee seh

Agree with
Slažem se sa
sla-zhem se sa

Scold
Grditi
grr-dee-tee

Argue
Rasprava
rah-sprah-vah

I don't agree
Ne slažem se
ne sla-zhem se

I agree with him / her
Slažem se sa njim / njom
sla-zhem se sa nee-im / Sla-zhem se sa n-yom

I disagree
Ne slažem se
ne sla-zhem se

Why are we arguing?
Zašto se raspravljamo?
zash-to se rah-sprav-lja-mo?

Useful Phrases and Structures

The Bosnian language, like English, features a rich set of useful phrases and structures that facilitate smooth communication. For instance, to greet someone in the morning, you'd say '**Dobro jutro**' in Bosnian, akin to 'Good morning' in English. Polite inquiries about well-being are captured in '**Kako se osjećaš?**' — 'How are you feeling?' in English. Expressing gratitude is similar in both languages, with '**Hvala**' in Bosnian translating to 'Thank you' in English. In terms of structure, Bosnian often places the verb at the end, in contrast to the typical Subject-Verb-Object structure in English. Take '**Ja čitam knjigu**' (I am reading a book) in Bosnian, where the verb '**čitam**' (am reading) falls in the middle.

First, firstly
Prvo
prr-vo

Then / later on
Onda / Kasnije
on-da / kah-snee-yeh

Again, still
Ponovo, ipak
poh-noh-vo, ee-pahk

Besides that / apart from that
Osim toga
o-seem toh-gah

Finally, in the end
Napokon, na kraju
nah-po-kon / na kra-yu

Let alone, despite
Kamoli, uprkos
ka-mo-lee, ooprkos

Instead of
Umjesto
oom-yeah-sto

Firstly, we disagree
Prvo, ne slažemo se
prr-vo, nee-smo se sla-ga-lee

Then, they quarrel
Onda, svađali su se
on-da, sva-đa-li soo se

I also disagree
Ja se također ne slažem
yah seh tah-koh-jer neh sla-jem

Verbs Expressing Your Thoughts

In the Bosnian language, verbs that express thoughts or opinions, such as '**mislim**' (I think) or '**vjerujem**' (I believe), are commonly used to convey personal views. These verbs are often placed at the end of sentences, like '**Ovo je dobro, mislim**' (This is good, I think). This contrasts with English, where such verbs usually appear at the start of sentences, as in 'I think this is good.' The order of verbs and subjects in Bosnian can create nuanced emphasis on the thought being expressed.

Think, imagine, conceive (meditate)
Misli, zamisli, shvati
mee-slee, zah-mee-slee, zah-mee-shlah-te

I have pondered over our argument
Razmišljao sam o našoj svađi
raz-mi-sh-l-yao sam o nash-o-ee svad-yi

Opinion
Mišljenje
meesh-lyen-yeh

Views, thoughts, ideas
Pogledi, misli, ideje
poh-gleh-dee, mee-slee, ee-deh-yeh

Feelings
Osjećaji
os-yeh-chai-yee

Fact, certainty
Činjenica, izvjesnost
cheen-yeh-nee-tsah, eez-vyehs-nost

Doubt
Sumnja
soom-nyah

Clear, evident, open, overt
Jasno, evidentno, otvoreno, očito
yahs-no, eh-vee-dehnt-no, ot-voh-reh-no, oh-chee-to

My feelings are clear
Moja osjećanja su jasna
mo-ya os-yeh-cha-nya soo yas-n

I don't like those ideas
Ne sviđaju mi se ove ideje
neh svee-dyah-noo mee se o-veh ee-deh-ye

Are you sure?

Jesi li siguran? – (Male)

ye-si lee see-goo-rahn?

Jesi li sigurna? – (Female)

ye-si lee see-goor-na?

It is a fact

To je činjenica

to yeh cheen-yeh-nee-tsah

There's no doubt

Nema sumnje

neh-mah soom-nyeh

Without doubt

Bez ikakve sumnje

bez ee-kahk-veh soom-nyeh

But, on the contrary, rather, but

Ali, naprotiv, radije, ali

ah-lee, nah-proh-teev, rah-dee-yeh, ah-lee

However

Kako god / Međutim

kah-koh god / meh-joo-tim

Full Sentence Examples

In Bosnian, expressing thoughts can be nuanced, often placing emphasis on the thought itself. For instance, '**Mislim da je ova knjiga zanimljiva**' translates to 'I think this book is interesting.' In contrast, in English, the emphasis often falls on the speaker, as in 'I believe this movie is fantastic.' Another example in Bosnian is '**Vjerujem da je on u pravu**,' translating to 'I believe he is right.' In English, we might say, 'I feel that she is mistaken.' Hence, while both languages provide means to express thoughts, the placement of verbs in Bosnian puts more focus on the thought, unlike English, where the emphasis is usually on the speaker.

You have some good ideas, but I don't agree with them
Imaš neke dobre ideje, ali ja se ne slažem s njima
imaš ne-ke do-bre i-de-je, a-li ja se ne sla-žem s nji-ma

However, I agree with their ideas
Međutim, ja se slažem s njihovim idejama
meh-joo-tim, yah seh slah-zhem s nyi-hov-im ee-deh-ya-ma

As for myself, I think all are right
Što se mene tiče, mislim da su svi u pravu
shto se me-ne ti-che, mis-lim da su svi u pra-vu

Even so, our views are different

Uprkos svemu, naši pogledi su različiti

oop-r-kos sveh-moo, nash-ee po-gle-dee soo raz-lee-chee-tee

Well-wishing

In Bosnian, well-wishing is often expressed through phrases like '**Sretno**' (Good luck) or '**Sve najbolje**' (All the best). These phrases focus on the recipient's fortune, underscoring the collective nature of Bosnian culture. In English, well-wishing often includes the speaker, as in 'I wish you luck' or 'I hope you do well.' This subtly places more emphasis on the well-wisher's intentions. For instance, in Bosnian, one might say, 'Sretno na ispitu' (Good luck on your exam), highlighting the exam's importance. In contrast, English speakers would say, 'I wish you luck on your exam,' emphasizing their personal hope for success.

Congratulations

Čestitke

che-stee-tke

To give someone congratulations

Čestitati nekome

che-stee-ta-tee ne-ko-meh

Happy birthday
Sretan rođendan
sreh-tahn roh-jen-dahn

We wish her luck for the new year
Želimo joj sreću za novu godinu
zhe-lee-mo yoy sre-tsu za no-vu go-dee-nu

Extending Invitations

In Bosnian culture, extending invitations often involves warm and welcoming phrases like '**Dođi kod nas na večeru**' ('Come to our place for dinner') or '**Da li bi željela izaći s nama večeras?**' ('Would you like to go out with us tonight?'). There's a strong emphasis on inclusivity and communal activities. In contrast, English invitations tend to be more direct and individualistic, such as 'Would you like to join me for dinner?' or 'Are you free to go to the movies tonight?'. The choice of words often reflects the societal norms and values of each language, with Bosnian emphasizing community and English valuing individualism.

Invite
Pozvati
poz-va-tee

Attend
Prisustvo
pree-soost-vo

Wedding invitation
Pozivnica za vjenčanje
poz-iv-nee-tsa za v-yen-chan-yeh

Accept an invitation
Prihvatiti pozivnicu
pree-hva-tee-tee poz-iv-nee-tsu

Party
Zabava
za-ba-va

Decline an invitation
Odbiti pozivnicu
od-bee-tee poz-iv-nee-tsu

Reception
Prijem
pree-yem

Example Statements Inviting Someone

In Bosnian, inviting someone is often imbued with warmth and community spirit. You might hear, '**Dođi na kafu, bit će nam lijepo**' ('Come for coffee, we'll have a good time'), emphasizing the shared enjoyment. On the other hand, in English, invitations can be more straightforward and personalized. For instance, 'Would you like to come for dinner?' focuses on the invitee's preference. While both languages extend an invitation, Bosnian emphasizes a collective experience, whereas English offers an individual choice, reflecting their respective cultural values of communal harmony and personal autonomy.

We are inviting you to the wedding

Pozivamo te na vjenčanje

poz-ee-va-mo te na v-yen-chan-yeh

He invited his friend for dinner

On je pozvao svog prijatelja na večeru

on ye poz-vao svog pree-ya-te-lja na ve-che-ru

I am sorry to inform you that I will not be able to attend the reception

Žao mi je što vas obavještavam, da neću biti u mogućnosti prisustvovati prijemu

zha-o mi ye shto vas o-bav-yeshtav-am da ne-chu bee-tee oo mo-guć-nos-tee pri-sust-vo-va-tee pri-ye-mu

The Hu Tense

In the Bosnian language, the 'hu' tense, used to describe recurring past actions, is often expressed using the auxiliary verb '**bi**' with the imperfective verb, for instance, '**On bi čitao**' (He used to read). The

English language, on the other hand, typically expresses the 'hu' tense with 'used to' or 'would' before the verb, e.g., 'He used to read' or 'He would read.' Both languages use this tense to convey past habits; however, the Bosnian language uses a single-word auxiliary, while English often employs a phrasal auxiliary. Regardless, the context and meaning remain similar, emphasizing past routines or habits.

I usually arrive

Ja obično stignem

ya obich-no stig-nem

You usually arrive

Ti obično stigneš

ti obich-no stig-neš

You usually arrive

Vi – (plural/formal)

obično stignete

vi obično stig-ne-te

They usually arrive

Oni obično stignu

o-nee obich-no stig-nu

She / He usually arrives

Ona / on obično stigne

o-na obich-no stig-ne / o-n obich-no stig-ne

Children usually arrive

Djeca obično stignu

dje-tsa obich-no stig-nu

We usually arrive

Mi obično stignemo

mi obično stig-ne-mo

The teacher usually arrives

Učitelj obično stigne

u-chee-te-ly obich-no stig-ne

This pattern continues throughout the noun classes:

The train (usually) arrives each day except Sundays
Voz obično stiže svaki dan osim nedjelje
voz obich-no sti-zhe sva-ki dan o-sim ne-dye-lje

The fruits (usually) arrive every week
Voće obično stiže svake sedmice
vo-tse obich-no sti-zhe sva-ke sed-mi-tse

New books (usually) arrive in the library at the end of
every month
**Nove knjige obično stižu u biblioteku na kraju
svakog mjeseca**
*No-ve knji-ge obich-no sti-zhu u bi-blio-te-ku na kra-ju sva-
kog mje-se-ca*

I usually eat
Ja obično jedem
ya obich-no ye-dem

I usually drink
Ja obično pijem
ya obich-no pee-yem

Present Tense

The present tense in Bosnian is used to express actions that are happening now or habitual actions, like English. However, Bosnian has a more complex conjugation system, with numerous forms depending on the subject. For example, '**čitam**' means 'I read' and '**čitate**' means 'you read.' In contrast, English uses the same verb form for all subjects except the third person singular. For instance, 'I read,' 'you read,' but 'he reads.' Additionally, Bosnian uses the present tense for future actions, unlike English. For example, '**Idem u park sutra**' literally translates to 'I go to the park tomorrow,' whereas in English, the future tense is used: 'I will go to the park tomorrow.' Despite these differences, both languages use the present tense to express current and habitual actions, showing similar usages in different linguistic contexts.

I am eating	They are going
Ja jedem	**Oni idu**
ya ye-dem	*o-nee ee-doo*
We are drinking	You are coming
Mi pijemo	**Ti dolaziš**
mi pee-yemo	*ti do-la-zish*

He / She is leaving
On / Ona odlazi
on od-la-zi / o-na od-la-zi

Negative Present Tense

In the Bosnian language, the negative present tense is created by adding the particle '**ne**' in front of the verb, like '**Ja ne čitam**' (I do not read). In contrast, English uses the auxiliary verb 'do' or 'does' not before the verb, as in 'I do not read' or 'He does not read.' Both languages use the negative present tense to express something that is not happening now or habitual actions that do not take place. However, Bosnian's negative form is a single word, whereas English's is phrasal. Another example is '**Ti ne pečeš**' (You do not bake) in Bosnian, compared to English's 'You do not bake.' Despite the structural differences, both languages succeed in conveying the same negative present tense meaning.

You usually think (Hu tense)
Ti obično misliš
ti obich-no mis-lish

I am not eating
Ja ne jedem
ya ne ye-dem

We are not drinking
Mi ne pijemo
mi ne pee-yemo

They are not going
Oni ne idu
o-nee ne ee-doo

You are not coming
Ti ne dolaziš
ti ne do-la-zish

He / She is not leaving
On / Ona ne odlazi
on ne od-la-zi / o-na ne od-la-zi

CHAPTER TWELVE:

ACTION VERBS

In the Bosnian language, 'action verbs' or '**glagoli radnje**' denote a physical or mental action. Like English, these verbs are vital in expressing activities. However, Bosnian verbs change form according to person, number, and tense, making them more complex than English verbs. For instance, the Bosnian verb '**čitati**' (to read) becomes '**čitam**' (I read), '**čitaš**' (you read), etc. In English, action verbs such as 'read' remain the same for all persons except for the third person singular in the present tense ('reads'). Despite the differences, both languages use action verbs to create dynamic sentences. For example, '**Igrati**' in Bosnian and 'Play' in English both denote an action of engaging in a game or activity. The sentence '**Ja igram fudbal**' in Bosnian translates to 'I play football' in

English, showing the similar usage of action verbs in both languages.

I sing	You read
Ja pjevam	**Ti čitaš**
ya pje-vam	*ti či-taš*
You run	He / She writes
Ti trčiš	**On / Ona piše**
ti tr-chiš	*on pee-she / o-na pee-she*
They eat	
Oni jedu	
o-nee ye-du	

Prefixes - Basics

This lesson provides the basic information needed for sentence construction. Prefixes in the Bosnian language play a significant role in the formation of words. As a Slavic language, Bosnian utilizes prefixes to change the meaning of words, often dramatically, providing a rich tapestry of expression. A common example of a Bosnian prefix is 'pre-', which implies an action done prematurely or excessively, as in '**preskočiti**' (to skip over) or '**pretjerati**' (to overdo).

On the other hand, the English language prefixes also modify the meaning of root words, but they are not as impactful as in Bosnian. English prefixes are generally used to create opposites or to quantify, like 'un-' in 'unhealthy' or 'bi-' in 'bicycle'. The meaning of an English word with a prefix is often predictable based on the meanings of its parts.

A key difference between the two languages is the usage of prefixes. In Bosnian, a prefix can drastically change the meaning of a word, sometimes creating a word with an entirely different concept. This is unlike English where prefixes mostly alter the degree or negate the root word's meaning.

Despite these differences, both languages leverage prefixes to expand vocabulary and expression. However, Bosnian prefixes offer a more nuanced and dynamic use, creating a wide range of meaning from a single root word.

To be able	To read
Moći	**Čitati**
mo-chi	*Či-ta-ti*

To buy
Kupiti
ku-pi-ti

To sell
Prodati
pro-da-ti

To remove
Izbrisati
iz-bri-sa-ti

To drink
Piti
pi-ti

To come
Doći
do-ći

To sit
Sjesti
s-yesti

To say
Reći
re-ći

To eat
Jesti
yesti

To cook
Kuhati
ku-ha-ti

To sleep
Spavati
spa-vah-tee

To see
Vidjeti
vid-ye-ti

To feel
Osjećati
os-yeh-cha-tee

To cry
Plakati
pla-ka-ti

To speak
Pričati
pree-cha-tee

To give
Dati
da-tee

To stand up
Istaknuti se
ees-tahk-nu-tee seh

To think
Misliti
mee-slee-tee

To go
Ići
ee-chee

To travel
Putovati
poo-toh-va-tee

To hear
Čuti
choo-tee

To wake up
Probuditi se
pro-boo-dee-tee seh

To laugh
Smijati se
smee-ya-tee seh

To walk
Hodati
ho-da-tee

To like / to love
Sviđati / Voljeti
svee-jah-tee / vol-yeh-te

To want
Željeti
zhel-yeh-tee

To listen
Slušati
sloo-sha-tee

To wash
Oprati
o-pra-tee

To look at
Pogledati u
po-gle-da-tee oo

To watch
Gledati
gle-da-tee

To look for
Tražiti
tra-zhee-tee

To work
Raditi
ra-dee-tee

To pay
Platiti
pla-tee-tee

To write
Pisati
pee-sa-tee

CHAPTER THIRTEEN:

OTHER USEFUL PHRASES

In the Bosnian language, '**korisne fraze**' or 'useful phrases' form an integral part of everyday communication, much like in English. These phrases provide a handy tool to navigate various social situations, express feelings, or request information. For instance, the Bosnian phrase '**Kako se zovete?**' translates to 'What is your name?' in English, a valuable question when meeting someone new. '**Molim vas**' in Bosnian is the English equivalent of 'Please,' a universal phrase demonstrating politeness. Another common phrase is '**Hvala**,' which translates to 'Thank you,' a fundamental expression of gratitude in any language.

Similarly, in English, useful phrases like 'How are you?' or 'Excuse me,' have their counterparts in

Bosnian as 'Kako ste?' and 'Izvinite,' respectively. Both languages use these phrases to foster smooth and respectful interactionss.

Excuse me	Where is the bathroom?
Izvinite	**Gdje je wc?**
iz-vee-nee-teh	*gdyeh yeh vet-seh*
How much does it cost?	What is your name?
Koliko košta?	**Kako se zoveš?**
ko-lee-ko kosh-ta	*kah-koh seh zoh-vehsh*

Food

Just like in English, the Bosnian language has a rich vocabulary for 'foods' or '**hrana**,' reflecting the country's diverse culinary tradition. A popular Bosnian dish, '**ćevapi**' (*che-vap-ee*), translates to small grilled sausages in English. '**Burek**,' a savory pastry filled with meat, is another staple, like a meat pie in English cuisine. Yet, some foods, like '**krompir**' (potatoes) and '**jabuka**' (apple), share universal recognition in both languages. Despite the language differences, the shared love for food, be it a hearty '**gulaš**' (goulash) in Bosnian or a comforting 'soup' in English, transcends cultural boundaries. Understanding these terminologies in both languages can enrich one's culinary experiences and appreciation for diverse cultures.

Food	Vegetables
Hrana	**Povrće**
hrah-nah	*poh-vr-cheh*
Bread	Fruit
Hljeb	**Voće**
lyeb	*vo-cheh*
Meat	Chicken
Meso	**Piletina**
meh-so	*pee-leh-tee-nah*
Fish	Corn
Riba	**Kukuruz**
ree-bah	*koo-rooz*

Other useful expression in this context includes

I am hungry
Gladan sam
glah-dahn sahm

What kind of food is there today?
Koja je vrsta hrane tu danas?
koy-ah yeh vr-stah hrah-neh too da-nas

Today, there are potatoes, meat, and fruit here
Danas su tu krompir, meso i voće
da-nas soo too krom-peer, meh-so ee vo-cheh

Can I get a salad?
Mogu li dobiti salatu?
mo-goo lee doh-bee-tee sah-la-to

Certainly sir, you will get it
Naravno gospodine, dobit ćete
Nah-rah-vno go-spo-dee-ne, do-bee-tse-te

Bring me some carrots
Donesi mi malo mrkve
ooh-neh-see mee mah-lo mrk-veh

Lamb
Ovčetina
ov-cheh-tee-nah

Beef
Govedina
go-veh-dee-nah

Pork
Svinjetina
svee-nyeh-tee-nah

Chicken
Piletina
pee-leh-tee-nah

Do you have roast meat here
Imate li pečeno meso ovdje
ee-mah-teh lee peh-cheh-no meh-so ov-dyeh

Yes, we have…
Da, imamo…
dah, ee-mah-mo

How much do you want?
Koliko želite?
Ko-lee-ko zheh-lee-teh

Do they put in onions and pepper?
Stavljaju li luk i biber?
stav-lja-ju lee look ee bee-ber?

Drinks

In Bosnian, 'drinks' are referred to as '**pića**,' showing the depth of the language's vocabulary. A few examples include '**kafa**' (coffee), '**čaj**' (tea), and '**sok**' (juice). Comparatively, in English, the terms are straightforward, without the characteristic diacritical marks of the Bosnian language. Also, there is a fascinating cultural aspect to these drinks. For instance, Bosnians often enjoy their '**kafa**' in a traditional manner, much like the English love for 'tea' with its own set of traditions. Understanding these nuances not only broadens our language skills but also provides a window into the cultures, enhancing our appreciation for global diversity.

Some people like to be refreshed having visited places holidays and so here are some of the expressions you may need:

Tea
Čaj
ch-ai

Orange squash / juice
Sok od narandže
sok od nah-ran-dje

Tea without milk
Čaj bez mlijeka
ch-ai bez m-lee-ye-ka

Hot milk
Vruće mlijeko
vroo-cheh m-lee-ye-ko

Coffee
Kafa
kah-fah

Cold
Hladno
hlahd-noh

Coffee without milk
Kafa bez mlijeka
kah-fah bez m-lee-ye-ka

One very cold beer
Jedno veoma hladno pivo
yed-no veh-o-ma hlad-no pee-vo

One warm beer
Jedno toplo pivo
yed-no toh-plo pee-vo

Soda with ice
Soda sa ledom
so-da sa leh-dom

Bring me cold water and whisky
Donesi mi hladnu vodu i viski
do-neh-see mee hlad-noo vo-doo ee vees-kee

What do you drink?
Šta piješ?
shta pee-ye-sh?

I am thirsty
Žedan sam – (Male)
zheh-dan sahm

Žedna sam – (Female)
zhehd-na sahm

Drinks / Beverages
Pića
pee-cha

Water
Voda
voh-dah

Milk
Mlijeko
m-lee-ye-ko

Beer / whisky
Pivo / Viski
pee-vo / vees-kee

Sparkling water
Kisela voda
kee-seh-la vo-dah

Asking the Time

In Bosnian, 'asking the time' is conveyed as '**pitati za vrijeme**,' which literally translates to 'ask for time.' Unlike English, in Bosnian, time is usually given in a 24-hour format, rather than the 12-hour format common in English. For instance, 15:00 is '**petnaest sati**,' not 'three in the afternoon.' To ask, 'What time is it?' you'd say '**Koliko je sati?**' in Bosnian, while in English, we'd simply ask, 'What time is it?' Interestingly, the Bosnian language often uses the word '**sati**' (hours) when referring to time, even when asking for minutes. Understanding these linguistic nuances can enrich our cross-cultural interactions.

What's the time?
Koliko je sati?
ko-lee-ko yeh sah-tee?

What time is it now?
Koliko je sati sada?
ko-lee-ko yeh sah-tee sah-dah?

The time is…
Sati je…
sah-tee yeh

The time now is…

Vrijeme sada je…

vree-yeh-me sah-dah yeh

The time now is seven o'clock in the evening / It is nineteen o'clock

Sada je sedam sati uveče / sada je "devetnaest" sati

sah-dah yeh se-dahm sah-tee oo-veh-cheh / sah-dah yeh de-veht-nahst sah-tee

The time now is twelve o'clock in the daytime (noon)

Sada je dvanaest sati u podne

sah-dah yeh dvah-na-est sah-tee oo pod-neh

Asking the date

In Bosnian, 'asking the date' translates to '**pitati za datum**.' For instance, if you want to ask, 'What's the date today?' you'd say '**Koji je danas datum?**' The date is announced in a day-month-year format, like '**dvadeset peti drugi dvije hiljade dvadeset i prve**' for '25th February 2021.' On the other hand, in English, the date can be asked simply as 'What's the date today?' and can be expressed in multiple formats, notably the month-day-year format in the US or the day-month-year format in many other English-speaking countries. These differences underscore the diverse ways in which the same information is communicated across languages.

What is the date today?

Koji je datum danas?

ko-yee yeh da-tum da-nas?

Today's date is…

Današnji datum je…

dah-nah-shnee da-toom yeh

Today is the sixteenth of November

Danas je šesnaesti novembar

dah-nas yeh shehs-nah-es-tee noh-vem-bar

Asking what somebody is doing

In the Bosnian language, asking what someone is doing is quite straightforward. You'd ask '**Šta radiš?**' which translates directly to 'What are you doing?' in English. Unlike in English, there's no need for the continuous tense in Bosnian, making it simpler.

What are you doing?

Šta radiš?

shta rah-deesh?

What are you doing?

Šta radite?

shta rah-dee-te?

I am eating

Jedem

yeh-dem

We are studying

Učimo

oo-chee-mo

Pronouns and copula

In Bosnian, pronouns and the copula verb '**je**' form the backbone of many sentences. Examples include '**On je dobar**' (He is good) and '**Ona je lijepa**' (She is beautiful). In English, pronouns and the copula verb 'is' function similarly, but there's more variation in the copula, depending on the subject. For instance, 'He is kind' and 'They are happy'. Both languages rely heavily on pronouns and the copula to construct meaningful sentences, but English uses a wider range of copulative verbs to accommodate its diverse subject pronouns.

I

Ja

yah

We

Mi

mee

You (Singular)	He / She
Ti	**On** / **Ona**
tee	*on* / *o-nah*
You (Plural)	They
Vi	**Oni**
vee	*o-nee*

Saying your nationality

In Bosnian, expressing your nationality is straight-forward. The phrase '**Ja sam**' followed by your nationality is used. For example, '**Ja sam Bosanac**' means 'I am Bosnian.' In English, the structure is similar, using 'I am' plus the nationality. For instance, 'I am American.' Both languages use the first-person singular pronoun and the copula, but in Bosnian, nationalities are typically not capitalized as they are in English. Furthermore, Bosnian language often expresses nationality in gendered forms, something not common in English. For example, '**Ja sam Bosanka**' denotes a Bosnian woman.

I am Swedesh	I am Japanese
Ja sam Šveđanin	**Ja sam Japanac**
yah sahm sh-veh-dyah-neen	*yah sahm yah-pah-nats*

I am French
Ja sam Francuz
yah sahm frahn-tsooz

I am Somalian
Ja sam Somalijac
yah sahm so-mah-lee-yats

I am German
Ja sam Nijemac
yah sahm nyeh-mats

I am an Indian
Ja sam Indijac
yah sahm in-dee-yats

Countries

Countries, or '**države**' in Bosnian, are referred to in a manner like English. However, in Bosnian, countries often have gendered forms, unlike in English. For instance, '**Bosna**' (Bosnia) is feminine, while '**Hrvatska**' (Croatia) is also feminine. In contrast, English simply uses the country's name without gendering it, like 'Bosnia' or 'Croatia.' Additionally, when referring to citizens of a country, Bosnian language often uses a different word, like '**Bosanac**' for a Bosnian person, whereas English typically adds 'an' or 'ian' to the country's name, like 'Bosnian.' These subtle differences highlight the rich cultural nuances embedded in language

America	Canada
Amerika	**Kanada**
ah-meh-ree-kah	*kah-nah-dah*
Holland	Czech Republic
Holandija	**Češka Republika**
hoh-lahn-dee-yah	*cheh-ska reh-poo-blee-kah*
Germany	Colombia
Njemačka	**Kolumbija**
nyeh-mahtch-kah	*ko-lum-bee-ya*
Belgium	China
Belgija	**Kina**
bel-gee-yah	*kee-nah*
Mozambique	Bosnia
Mozambik	**Bosna**
moh-zahm-beek	*bos-nah*

Asking where someone comes from

In Bosnian, when asking where someone comes from, you would say '**Odakle si**?' for informal situations or '**Odakle ste**?' for formal ones. In English, you'd ask 'Where are you from?' The structure is similar, but Bosnian distinguishes between formal and informal situations. For instance, if someone is from Bosnia, they would reply '**Ja sam iz Bosne**' in Bosnian or 'I am from Bosnia' in English. If they are from the United States, they would say '**Ja sam iz Sjedinjenih Američkih Država**' or 'I am from the United States' in English. The responses are direct translations, highlighting the universality of this question.

Where do you come from? (Singular)
Odakle si?
o-dah-kle see?

Where do you come from? (Plural)
Odakle ste?
o-dah-kle steh?

Saying where you are stay / where you reside

In the Bosnian language, expressing where you reside is typically phrased as 'Ja živim u...,' followed by your place of residence. For instance, 'Ja živim u maloj kući' (I live in a small house), or 'Ja živim u studentskom domu' (I live in a university dorm). In contrast, in English, we articulate it as 'I live in...,' followed by the location. For example, 'I live in a small house' or 'I live in a university dorm'. Despite minor structural differences, both languages effectively communicate the concept of residence, emphasizing the individual's living environment rather than specific geographical locations.

I am staying at the university
Odsjedam na univerzitetu
od-syeh-dam na oo-nee-vehr-zi-teh-too

I am staying in a big building
Odsjedam u velikoj zgradi
od-syeh-dam oo veh-lee-koy zgra-dee

I am residing in a fine house
Odsjedam u finoj kući
od-syeh-dam oo fee-noy koo-chee

I am staying in a small house
Odsjedam u maloj kući
I am staying in a small house

I am staying at a hotel
Odsjedam u hotelu
od-syeh-dam oo ho-teh-loo

I am staying at home
Ostajem u kući
o-sta-yem oo koo-chee

I am living in a village
Živim na selu
zhee-veem na seh-loo

I am living in town
Živim u gradu
zhee-veem oo grah-doo

Saying where you live

In Bosnian, expressing where you live is typically phrased as '**Ja živim u**...,' followed by your location. For instance, if you live in Sarajevo, you would say '**Ja živim u Sarajevu**.' Comparatively, in English, you would say 'I live in...,' followed by your location. For example, if you reside in London, you would state 'I live in London.' Both languages employ the verb 'live' to denote residence, but Bosnian frequently integrates prepositions into the verb form, whereas English usually keeps them separate.

I live in Mombasa
Živim u Mombasi
zhee-veem oo Mom-bah-see

I live in a hotel
Živim u hotelu
Zhee-veem oo ho-teh-loo

I live in Tanzania
Živim u Tanzaniji
zhee-veem oo Tan-za-nee-yee

I live in a big building
Živim u velikoj zgradi
zhee-veem oo veh-lee-koy zgra-dee

I live in America
Živim u Americi
zhee-veem oo a-me-ree-tsee

I live in a fine house
Živim u finoj kući
zhee-veem oo fee-noy koo-chee

I live at home	I live in an apartment
Živim u kući	**Živim u apartmanu**
zhee-veem oo koo-chee	*zhee-veem oo a-par-tma-noo*

Describing your means of transportation

In Bosnian, when describing your means of transportation, you might say '**Ja se vozim**...' followed by the type of transportation. For instance, '**Ja se vozim biciklom**' (I ride a bicycle), or '**Ja se vozim autobusom**' (I ride a bus). In English, this would be phrased as 'I travel by...' followed by the type of transportation. For example, 'I travel by bicycle' or 'I travel by bus.' Both languages articulate the concept of transportation effectively, with Bosnian focusing on the verb '**vozim**' (ride) and English using 'travel by' to describe the mode of transportation.

I come on foot	I come by minibus
Dolazim pješke	**Dolazim minibusem**
doh-lah-zeem p-yesh-ke	*doh-lah-zeem mee-nee-boo-sehm*

I travel on foot
Putujem pješke
poo-too-yem p-yesh-ke

I travel by car
Putujem autom
poo-too-yem ow-tom

I travel by minibus
Putujem minibusom
poo-too-yem mee-nee-boo-sohm

I travel by train
Putujem vozom
poo-too-yem voh-zom

I travel by bus
Putujem autobusom
poo-too-yem ow-toh-boo-sohm

Feeling hungry, thirsty, or satisfied

In Bosnian, expressing states of hunger, thirst, or satisfaction involves verbs of feeling like '**osjećam se**' followed by an adjective. For example, '**osjećam se gladan**' means 'I feel hungry,' '**žedan sam/gladan sam**' translates to 'I feel thirsty,' and '**osjećam se zadovoljan**' equates to 'I feel satisfied.' In English, it works similarly, where 'I feel' is followed by the adjective describing the state. However, in casual conversation, English speakers often drop the 'I feel' part and simply state 'I'm hungry,' 'I'm thirsty,' or 'I'm satisfied.' Similar colloquial shortcuts may also be used in Bosnian, such as '**gladan sam**,' '**žedan sam**,' or '**zadovoljan sam**.'

See / feel
Vidjeti / Osjećati
vee-dyeh-tee / o-syeh-cha-tee

Hear / feel
Čuti / Osjećati
choo-tee / o-syeh-cha-tee

Examples:

I feel hungry
Osjećam se gladan
o-syeh-cham seh glah-dan

I am hungry
Gladan sam
glah-dan sahm

I am thirsty
Žedan sam
zheh-dan sahm

I'm satisfied, I've had enough
Zadovoljan sam, imao sam dovoljno
zah-doh-vo-lyan sahm, ee-ma-o sahm doh-volj-no

I am full
Pun sam
poon sahm

Making comparisons

Making comparisons in Bosnian and English share similar structures but with distinct verbiage. In Bosnian, to say something is better, you'd use '**bolji je**' before the noun, while in English, 'is better' follows the noun. For instance, '**Bosanska kafa je bolja od engleske**' translates to 'Bosnian coffee is better than English.' Similarly, to express something is less, Bosnians say '**manje je**' before the noun, while English speakers say 'is less' after the noun. For example, '**Manje je hladno u Bosni nego u Engleskoj**' means 'It's less cold in Bosnia than in England.' These subtle differences add unique flavor to each language.

Reading is as hard as cultivating
Čitanje je teško kao i kultivisanje
chee-ta-nye yeh tehsh-ko kah-o ee kul-tee-vee-sahn-yeh

Our father is as short as me
Naš otac je nizak kao i ja
nash oh-tats yeh nee-zak kah-o ee yah

There is less traffic today than it was yesterday
Manje je prometno danas nego juče
man-yeh yeh pro-met-no da-nas ne-go yoo-che

Describing an illness

Describing an illness in Bosnian involves detailing symptoms using verbs conjugated in the first person. For instance, '**Osjećam se bolesno**' translates to 'I feel sick.' Likewise, '**Imam visoku temperaturu**' means 'I have a high temperature.' In English, similar structures are used, but the verb 'to be' often replaces 'to have' for certain symptoms. For example, 'I am nauseous' instead of 'I have nausea.' Moreover, English speakers commonly use adjectives to describe their state directly, like 'I'm sick' or 'I'm unwell.' Both languages use descriptive language to convey the severity and nature of the illness.

I am sick
Bolestan sam – (Male)
boh-leh-stan sahm

Bolesna sam – (Female)
boh-les-na sahm

I have a fever
Imam groznicu
ee-mam groz-nee-tsoo

I have a cold
Prehlađen sam – (Male)
preh-lah-dyen sahm

Prehlađena sam –
(Female)
preh-lah-dyeh-na sahm

I am in pain
U bolu sam
oo boh-loo sahm

I have a stomachache
Imam bolove u stomaku
ee-mam bo-lo-ve oo sto-ma-koo

I have a headache
Imam glavobolju
ee-mam glah-vo-boh-l-yu

Describing how you feel

When describing feelings in Bosnian, you often use the verb '**osjećam se**' (I feel) followed by an adjective, such as '**osjećam se sretno**' (I feel happy). In contrast, in English, you typically use the verb 'to feel' before the adjective, as in 'I feel happy.' However, English also allows for more descriptive expressions like 'I'm on top of the world.' For instance, while in Bosnian you might say '**Osjećam se kao da sam na vrhu svijeta**' (I feel as if I'm on top of the world), the English version is more succinct and metaphorical. Both languages, thus, enable rich emotional expression.

Feel	Heat
Osjećati	**Vruće**
o-syeh-cha-tee	*vroo-che*

Cold	
Hladno	
hla-dno	

Examples in Dialogue

I feel cold	I feel hot
Hladno mi je	**Vruće mi je**
hla-dno mee yeh	*vroo-che mee yeh*

The body

In Bosnian, the body is referred to as 'tijelo,' and its parts are described with specific words. For example, 'ruka' is used for hand, 'noga' for leg, 'oči' for eyes, and 'uši' for ears. Just like English, Bosnian also has a vast vocabulary that allows for detailed descriptions of these body parts, such as 'prsti' (fingers), 'koljeno' (knee), or 'pluća' (lungs). Despite the differences in the languages, both Bosnian and English are equipped to describe the body and its parts in detail. The primary difference lies in the phonetic and syntactic structure of the languages, which leads to different word forms and sentence structures. For instance, the phrase 'I broke my leg' translates to 'Slomio sam nogu' in Bosnian, where the verb comes before the object, unlike English. However, the essence of meaning remains the same, demonstrating the universal nature of human anatomy language.

Parts of the body	Head
Dijelovi tijela	**Glava**
dee-yeh-lo-vee tee-yeh-la	*glah-vah*

Throat
Grlo
gr-lo

Neck
Vrat
vraht

Chest
Grudi
groo-dee

Shoulder
Ramena
rah-meh-na

Back
Leđa
leh-dya

Armpit
Pazušna jama
pah-zoo-shna ya-ma

Stomach
Stomak
stoh-mak

Elbow
Lakat
la-kat

Thumb
Palac
pah-lats

Arm
Ruka
roo-kah

Palm of Hand
Dlan ruke
dlan roo-keh

Forearm
Podlaktica
pod-lak-tee-tsah

Waist
Struk
strook

Wrist
Ručni zglob
roo-ch-nee zglob

Hip	Ankle
Kuk	**Nožni zglob**
kook	*nozh-nee zglob*
Hand	Knee
Ruka	**Koljeno**
roo-kah	*kol-yeh-no*
Fist	Foot
Šaka	**Stopalo**
shah-kah	*sto-pa-lo*
Finger	Heel
Prst	**Peta**
prst	*peh-ta*
Buttocks	Toe
Zadnjica	**Nožni palac**
zad-nee-tsa	*nozh-nee pah-lats*
Leg	Sole of foot
Noga	**Potplat stopala**
no-ga	*pot-plat sto-pa-la*
Thigh	Nail
Butina	**Nokat**
boo-tee-na	*no-kat*

CHAPTER FOURTEEN:

ACTIVITIES

In Bosnia, activities often differ from those in the English language. For instance, while it's common in English to use phrases like 'sports,' 'hobbies,' or 'pastimes' to describe activities, in the Bosnian language, expressions like '**zabava**,' '**rekreacija**,' or '**hobi**' are often used. These phrases highlight the sense of fun and relaxation in activities. For example, instead of simply saying 'I like to play football' as in English, in Bosnian, you could say '**Uživam u nogometu kao svom omiljenom hobiju**' (I enjoy football as my favorite hobby).

Another difference between Bosnian and English is the use of verbal forms for describing activities. Bosnian has a larger number of verb categories used for different types of activities. For instance, to describe sports activities, the verbal form '**sportski**' would be used, while for describing artistic activities, the verbal form '**umjetnički**' would be used. This diversity allows for a more precise expression of different types of activities in Bosnian.

When it comes to English, specific expressions are often used to describe certain activities. For instance, English has the expression 'water sports' to describe activities like surfing, kiteboarding, or diving. These are activities that are very specific to the English-speaking region and don't find the same extent in Bosnian.

In summary, while the concept of 'activities' is present in both Bosnian and English, the manner of expression and used phrases differ. Bosnian puts more emphasis on fun, relaxation, and the use of specific verbal forms for describing activities, while English uses specific expressions to describe certain activities not found in Bosnian.

Walk	Run
Šetati	**Trčati**
sheh-ta-tee	*tr-cha-tee*

Swim
Plivati
plee-va-tee

Dance
Plesati
ple-sa-tee

Read
Čitati
chee-ta-tee

Write
Pisati
pee-sa-tee

Cook
Kuhati
koo-ha-tee

Travel
Putovati
poo-toh-va-tee

Play (a game)
Igrati (igru)
ee-gra-tee

Paint
Slikati
slee-ka-tee

Sing
Pjevati

Listen (to music)
Slušati (muziku)
sloo-sha-tee moo-zee-koo

Shop
Kupovati
koo-po-va-tee

Climb
Penjati se
pen-ya-tee se

Explore
Istraživati
is-tra-zhee-va-tee

Hike
Planinariti
pla-nee-na-ree-tee

Cycle
Biciklirati
bee-tsee-klee-ra-tee

Fish
Ribariti
ree-bah-ree-tee

Photograph
Fotografisati
fo-to-gra-fee-sa-tee

Sightsee
Razgledati
rahz-gle-da-tee

CHAPTER FIFTEEN:

MINI ENGLISH/BOSNIAN TRAVEL DICTIONARY (A-Z)

Having an English-Bosnian mini dictionary at your disposal when visiting Bosnia is like a passport to a more immersive and rewarding travel experience. Understanding the local language can bridge the gap between feeling like an outsider and becoming part of the community, even if it's temporary. A dictionary can help you navigate through the city, order food in a restaurant, or ask for directions, making your journey smoother and more comfortable. It can also empower you to connect with the locals on a deeper level, enabling you to delve beneath the surface of tourist attractions and discover the hidden gems of Bosnian culture. Not to mention, it can save you from confusing situations or potential misunderstandings.

Therefore, an English-Bosnian mini dictionary is an essential companion for a fulfilling and enriching Bosnian adventure. It's not just about convenience; it's about truly experiencing the charm of Bosnia.

A

Adventure
Avantura
a-van-too-ra

Airport
Aerodrom
aero-drom

B

Backpack
Ruksak
rooks-uhk

Beach
Plaža
pla-zha

Baggage
Prtljag
prt-l-yag

Beer
Pivo
pi-vo

Bank
Banka
ban-ka

Bill
Račun
ra-chun

Bath
Kupatilo
ku-pa-tilo

Breakfast
Doručak
do-ru-chak

Bus
Autobus
au-to-bus

C

Cancellation
Otkazivanje
ot-ka-zee-vahn-ye

Cancelled
Otkazano
ot-ka-zano

Cathedral
Katedrala
ka-te-dra-la

Cave
Pećina
peh-chee-na

Check out
Odjava
od-ya-va

Check-in
Prijava
pree-yah-va

Church
Crkva
tsrk-va

City map
Gradski plan
grad-skee plan

Cliff
Klif
klif

Coffee
Kafa
ka-fa

Currency exchange
Mjenjačnica
myen-yach-nee-tsa

Customs
Carina
tsa-ree-na

D

Delayed
Odloženo
od-lo-zhe-no

Dinner
Večera
ve-che-ra

Desert
Pustinja
poost-een-ya

E

Eco-friendly
Ekološki
e-ko-losh-kee

Exchange
Razmjena
raz-mye-na

Emergency
Hitna situacija
heet-na see-too-ah-tsee-ya

F

Flight
Let
let

Food
Hrana
hra-na

Flight delay
Kašnjenje leta
kash-nyen-ye le-ta

Forest
Šuma
shoo-ma

G

Gluten-free
Bez glutena
bez gloo-te-na

Guide
Vodič
vo-di-ch

H

Help
Pomoć
po-mo-ch

Hospital
Bolnica
bol-nee-tsa

Hiking
Planinarenje
pla-nee-na-ren-ye

Hostel
Hostel
hoh-stel

Hotel
Hotel
ho-tel

I

Insurance
Osiguranje
oh-see-goo-rahn-ye

Itinerary
Plan putovanja
plahn poo-toh-vah-nyah

Island
Otok
o-tok

J

Jaywalk
Pretrčavati cestu
preh-truh-chah-va-tee tseh-stu

Jet ski
Džet-ski
dzhet-skee

K

Kayaking
Kajakaštvo
kay-ya-kash-tvo

L

Lake
Jezero
ye-ze-ro

Landmark
Znamenitost
zna-me-nee-tost

Lost property
Izgubljena imovina
eez-goo-blye-na ee-mo-vee-na

Lunch
Ručak
ru-chak

M

Map
Karta
kar-ta

Market
Pijaca
pi-ya-tsa

Menu
Meni
me-ni

Money
Novac
no-vats

Monument
Spomenik
spo-meh-neek

Mosque
Džamija
dja-mi-ya

Mountain range
Planinski lanac
pla-nee-skee la-nats

Museum
Muzej
moo-zey

N

National Park
Nacionalni park
natsio-nal-nee park

Natural attraction
Prirodna privlačnost
pree-rohd-na pree-vla-chnost

Network – (Business)
Veza
ve-za

Network – (Road network)
Mreža
mreh-zha

Nonstop
Neprekidno
neh-preh-keed-no

O

One-way trip
Put u jednom smijeru
poot oo yed-nom sm-yeh-roo

Online connection
Internetska veza
in-ter-net-ska ve-za

Outsource
Unajmljivanje stranih radnika
oo-nai-mlee-va-nye stra-nee rad-nee-ka

P

Passport
Pasoš
pa-so-sh

Pharmacy
Apoteka
a-po-te-ka

Police
Policija
po-li-tsi-ya

Police station
Policijska stanica
po-lee-tsee-yska sta-nee-tsa

Postcard
Razglednica
raz-gled-nee-tsa

Q

Quarantine
Karantin
kah-rahn-teen

Queue
Red
rehd

Quota
Kvota
kvo-ta

R

Reservation
Rezervacija
re-zer-va-tsi-ya

Restaurant
Restoran
resto-ran

Restaurant reservation
Rezervacija restorana
rez-er-va-tsee-ya res-to-ra-na

River
Rijeka
ree-ye-ka

Room
Soba
so-ba

S

Sea view
Pogled na more
poh-gled na mo-re

Shopping
Kupovina
ku-po-vi-na

Sightseeing
Razgledanje
raz-gle-dahn-ye

Snorkeling
Ronjenje
ron-yen-ye

Soap
Sapun
sa-pun

Souvenir
Suvenir
soo-ve-neer

Station
Stanica
sta-ni-tsa

Sunrise
Izlazak sunca
eez-la-zak soon-tsa

Sunset
Zalazak sunca
za-la-zak soon-tsa

T

Taxi
Taksi
tak-si

Taxi rank
Taksi stajalište
tak-see stay-ah-leesh-the

Ticket
Karta
kar-ta

Tip
Napojnica
na-po-y-ni-tsa

Toilet
WC
ve-tse

Tour guide
Vodič
vo-deech

Tourist
Turista
tur-ist-a

Towel
Peškir
pe-shkir

Traffic jam
Gužva u saobraćaju
goozh-va oo sah-oh-bra-cha-yoo

Train
Voz
Voz

U

Universal Time
Univerzalno vrijeme
oo-nee-veh-rzal-no vree-yeh-meh

Umbrella
Kišobran
kee-sho-brahn

Undeveloped
Neizgrađen
n-ay-ez-grah-dyen

Upgrade
Poboljšati
poh-boh-lye-sha-tee

V

Valley
Dolina
do-lee-na

Vegetarian
Vegetarijanac
ve-ge-ta-ri-ya-nats

Visa
Viza
vee-za

W

Water
Voda
vo-da

Waterfall
Vodopad
vo-do-pad

Wildlife
Divlji život
dee-vlyee zhee-vot

Wine
Vino
vi-no

X

Xmas (Christmas)
Božić
boh-zheech

Y

Yacht
Jahta
yahk-tah

Z

zip code
Poštanski broj
posh-tahn-skee broy

Zoo
Zološki vrt
zoh-oh-lohsh-kee vrt

CONCLUSION

As we draw the curtains on this enlightening journey through the English-Bosnian Dictionary, it's time to reflect on the key takeaways and the profound impact of this resource in bridging the linguistic gap between English and Bosnian speakers. In this comprehensive guide, we've delved into the depths of the Bosnian language—its nuances, unique expressions, and rich vocabulary. From the intricate expression of feelings to the detailed description of body parts, this book has illuminated the distinct characteristics of the Bosnian language, making it more accessible to English speakers.

The primary goal of this book has been to introduce the Bosnian language to English speakers, and we believe we have achieved this. It has served as a beacon, guiding language enthusiasts, students, educators, and casual learners through the complexities and beauties of Bosnian. By doing so, we have not only expanded their linguistic horizons but also opened the doors to a new culture, fostering a sense of understanding and camaraderie between diverse cultures.

Language is a powerful tool — a bridge that connects individuals, societies, and cultures, fostering mutual respect and understanding. In a world that continues to grow more diverse, the ability to communicate in more than one language is not just a skill but a necessity. This book, we hope, has played a crucial role in promoting this inclusivity, enabling effective communication, and establishing an atmosphere of mutual respect and understanding.

Furthermore, we have underscored the importance of language learning, emphasizing its role in personal growth, professional development, and social integration. It is our sincere hope that this book has sparked your interest in the Bosnian language and culture, inspiring you to continue exploring and learning.

In conclusion, this English-Bosnian Dictionary stands as a testament to the beauty of linguistic diversity and the power of language in fostering cultural exchange. It is more than just a book; it is a tool for empowerment, a catalyst for change, and a symbol of unity in diversity. As we close this chapter, we look forward to the countless conversations, connections, and cultural exchanges this book will inspire.

May this book serve as your trusted companion on your language-learning journey, inspiring you to continue exploring, understanding, and respecting the diverse world of languages.

REVIEW

This book has been created with immense passion, with the primary goal of bringing English speakers closer to Bosnian culture through the richness of its language. It's a portable tool that allows you to experience the enchanting world of Bosnian wherever you go. More than a mere dictionary, it serves as an open invitation to explore and genuinely appreciate the depth of Bosnian language and culture. Undoubtedly, it's an essential resource for language learners.

That said, we hope you relish the opportunity to delve into the intricacies of the Bosnian language and culture through our book. Your feedback is of immense value to us! If you've found the content informative and beneficial, we kindly invite you to consider leaving a review on Amazon. Your insights can be a guiding light for fellow language enthusiasts. Thank you for joining us on this journey of promoting linguistic diversity and fostering mutual understanding. Happy reading!

Made in the USA
Columbia, SC
09 November 2023

25822070R00091